PROMPT ENGINEERING THE SUBCONSCIOUS

DEBUG THE MIND THAT'S DEBUGGING YOUR BUSINESS

Anuraag Jain

For permissions and rights enquiries:
www.linkedin.com/in/anuraagjain

Disclaimer This book is intended for educational and informational purposes only. The frameworks, protocols, and methodologies described represent the author's experience and research. They do not constitute medical, psychological, or therapeutic advice. Readers experiencing mental health concerns should seek qualified professional support. The author and publisher accept no liability for outcomes arising from the application of content in this book. NLP techniques referenced in this book are drawn from established methodologies within the field of Neuro-Linguistic Programming. The author holds a Licensed Practitioner certification in NLP (Richard Bandler lineage, AlphaStars Academy) and an ICF-Approved Level 2 Executive Coaching certification.

ISBN: 978-1-0676926-0-5, 978-1-0676926-1-2, 978-1-0676926-2-9
Ebook edition also available.
Printed and distributed worldwide.
ISBNs
978-1-0676926-0-5 - PETS e-book
978-1-0676926-1-2 - PETS Paper Back
978-1-0676926-2-9 - PETS Hard Cover

Wherever this journey takes us,
Anuraag Jain

About the Author

Anuraag is a Fractional CTO, AI workflow architect, and high-performance executive coach with over twenty-nine years of experience scaling production platforms. Known as the Original AI (Anuraag's Intelligence), he built his career by entering the tech industry without a computer science degree. He took massive risks that guided companies like Betfair and The Hut Group to staggering 1.6 billion and 5.4 billion pound public offerings.

As the Founder of Growth Variable, he designs secure local AI architectures and conducts strategic AI audits for professional firms. He has directly trained over one hundred and forty leaders in applied AI to accelerate delivery.

After experiencing a profound plateau and debugging his own internal programming, he synthesized his licensed neuro-linguistic programming methodologies with AI architecture to create Technical Manifestation. Today, he teaches founders and executives how to prompt engineer their subconscious minds to scale their businesses.

Dedication

To the visionaries sitting in the waiting room of belief. The latency period is over.

To my family, who formed the foundation of the Original AI.

To my parents, who gave rise to the system that would eventually be engineered.

To my wife, daughter, and sister, who monitored the system even when the screen was dark and when my perception was unstable.

To my siblings and their partners, who participated in the early testing and refinement of this framework.

To my extended family, elders, teachers, mentors, coaches, and clients, who provided the constraints, feedback, and training data that shaped this system.

Special mention to Sidhharrth S Kumaar, my guru, who consistently pushed me to bring this work into the world.

To Sat and Siri Khalsa, whose teaching of coaching helped me recognise and structure the patterns within this system.

To my fellow coaches, who challenged, refined, and strengthened my thinking.

And to the fellow student code-named "RAG", who read every iteration of this work and helped bring it to completion.

Table of Contents

Introduction:
THE WAITING ROOM OF BELIEF

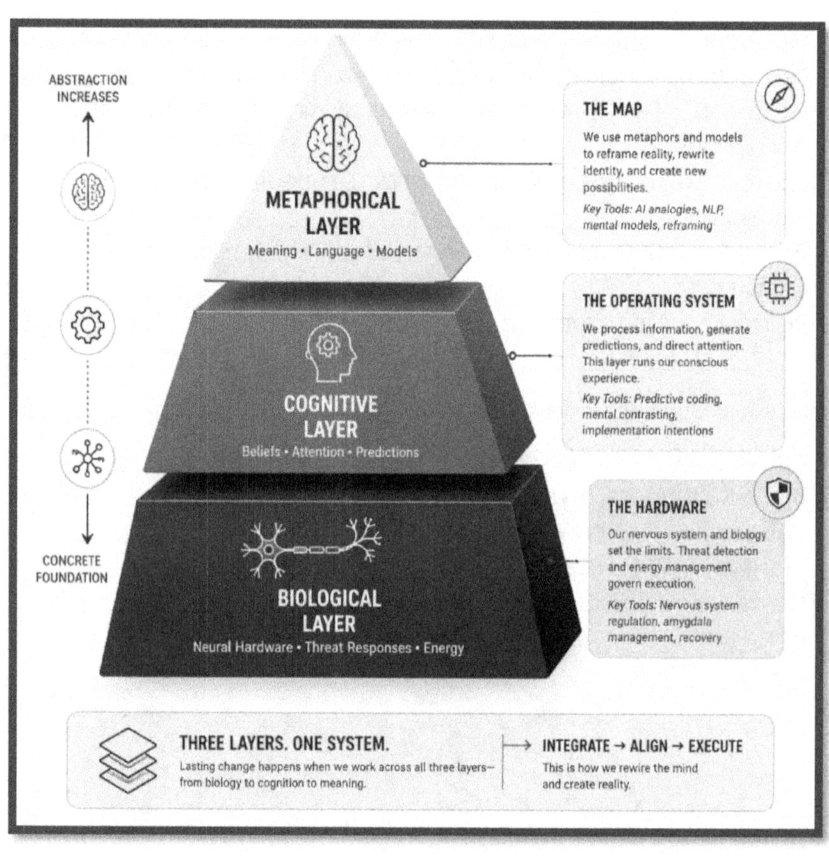

The Compiled Reality

I close my eyes and see my future clearly. I sit in my stone manor, looking out from my office toward the greenhouse, the fountain, the koi. The vision is fully rendered. When I open my eyes, I look at my computer screen. The physical manifestation of that stone manor is my active vision. My current reality is optimized and far beyond where I started. The financial hurdles that once stalled my progress have been successfully debugged. My enterprise generates steady momentum. My predictable trajectory is set. I operate from this state of internal knowingness to generate the exact reality I desire. My past struggles were useful diagnostic data. These temporary bugs provided the exact training data required to engineer a flawless execution engine.

The Invisible Ceiling

This API documentation is for the high-performing founder and the ambitious executive. You scale your impact. You know you are meant for more. You possess the intelligence and the drive. Yet you hit an invisible ceiling. Something holds you back. Brilliant professionals frequently hit these invisible ceilings and freeze. They sit in the waiting room of belief.

You stare at a massive goal and experience a sudden inability to execute. You delay the email. You overthink the proposal. You refine your work instead of shipping it. You assume you lack discipline. You attempt to force your physical execution through sheer willpower. Intelligent professionals consistently misdiagnose this biological hardware failure as a character flaw. They label it imposter syndrome or laziness. They are completely wrong. Perfectionism is not a personality trait. It is a latency strategy deployed by your brain to delay exposure. Your system is not confused. It is running an identity protection protocol.

The Architectural Metaphor

I immersed myself in the mechanics of Artificial Intelligence. I built multi-agent workflows. I engineered prompts for Large Language Models. A profound realization struck me during this process. I looked in a metaphorical mirror and saw the exact architecture of human limitation.

When you give an AI a complex query without a clear objective, it suffers from context saturation. Its processing power overloads. The machine cannot calculate a safe path forward. Lacking strict parameters, it panics. It hallucinates a false reality based on bad data. It generates garbage.

The human mind behaves in exact accordance with this structural logic. When you feed your brain a massive, undefined goal, you overflow your active working memory. You trigger a severe threat response. You sit in the waiting room because your internal operating system is overloaded. In simple terms, when your brain cannot see a clear next step, it assumes danger and shuts down. A highly effective way to model our cognition is through the architectural logic of AI prompt engineering.

The Three-Layer Architecture

Before we rewrite your base code, we must establish the operational parameters. Comparing the human mind to an AI is a high-performance abstraction. It provides a schematic to bypass your conscious resistance. To build a highly effective execution engine, this framework operates across three distinct layers.

The Biological Layer. This covers your neural hardware and your biological threat responses. Research indicates that our frontostriatal network and our amygdala hijack our physical execution when overloaded. We model this as a physical hardware failure. When your brain exceeds its cognitive compute limit, it triggers an adaptive self-protective mechanism. It shuts down your motivation to conserve caloric energy. You do not have a motivation problem. You have a token limit error.

The Cognitive Layer: This dictates your beliefs and your active attention. This layer manages predictive coding and mental contrasting. The brain is a prediction machine. It continuously matches incoming sensory data against its internal expectations. If you attempt to force a new identity without updating these expectations, your brain registers a prediction error. Your conscious firewall blocks the new code. We use specific cognitive protocols to drop this firewall and install the update.

The Metaphorical Layer. Here we map these mental processes directly onto AI architecture. We use concepts like context drift, semantic chunking, and multi-agent orchestration. We translate literal AI prompting mechanics into neuro-linguistic programming exercises. These exercises directly rewrite your subconscious model weights.

Two Paths of Entry

This framework was built for two very different kinds of minds. Both arrive at the same destination.

If you have never written a line of code in your life, this book was designed with you in mind first. You do not need to understand artificial intelligence. You do not need to know what a large language model is. Every technical term in this text is a precisely chosen metaphor — a new language for an old problem. That problem is this: the standard vocabulary of self-help has stopped working on you. Words like *mindset, limiting beliefs* and *manifestation* have been overused to the point of invisibility. You have read the books. You have attended the seminars. You still hit the ceiling.

The language of computing strips away that accumulated emotional weight. When you read that your brain has hit a *token limit*, something clicks that *overwhelm* never quite managed. When you understand that your self-doubt is a *corrupted system prompt* running silently in the background, you stop treating it as a character flaw and start treating it as an engineering problem. Engineering problems have solutions. You already knew that.

Read every technical term the way you would read a well-chosen metaphor in a novel. You do not need to know how a compass works to follow one north.

If you are a technical reader — an engineer, an architect, a CTO — you will notice something unusual here. The metaphors are precise. They are not the lazy approximations that litter most business books. *Context drift, semantic chunking, multi-agent orchestration, vector re-indexing* — these terms are not borrowed for effect. They are applied with structural accuracy to the cognitive science they describe. You will recognise the logic immediately, because it is the same logic you use to diagnose production failures at 2 am.

The shift this book asks of you is a single one: turn that diagnostic intelligence inward. The system you have spent your career building and scaling is not just the platform. It is you.

The Compiled Output: What You Will Execute

This text is API documentation. When you install these protocols, your internal architecture fundamentally changes. You stop attempting to fix a hardware problem with a motivational quote. Willpower is finite and unscalable. Relying on sheer manual effort to force your physical execution is an architectural failure. You are going to write a new prompt to compile specific, measurable outputs in the physical world.

Here is the exact code you will install to rewrite your operating system.

Hack the Biological Threat Response. Stop triggering your amygdala with massive, undefined goals. You will learn to use Retroactive Prompting to trick your neural hardware into a safe state. By framing your overarching vision as a safely completed historical fact, you engage your prefrontal cortex. You bypass the amygdala's threat response. You retrieve your success blueprint directly from your Distributed Intelligence (your brain's latent pattern-recognition systems).

Clear Context Saturation: Eliminate the paralysis of perfectionism and overthinking. You will shrink your daily execution into microscopic one-minute tokens. This strict architectural constraint directly bypasses the biological giving-up strategy. You drop your cognitive load below the threshold of fear to guarantee immediate physical momentum.

Deploy Multi-Agent Workflows. Stop trying to solve massive corporate problems using a single panicked processor. You will map your internal Board of Directors. You will orchestrate specialized internal personas to resolve deadlocks. You will distribute your cognitive load to maintain absolute calm under intense executive pressure.

Re-index Your Biological Vector Database. Execute a twenty-four-hour Discovery Scan. Command your Reticular Activating System to filter out environmental noise. Stop acting as a passive background processor. You will actively retrieve the exact leading indicators and strategic resources required to compile your vision in the physical world.

Automate Your Cognitive Infrastructure. Stop relying on manual daily effort. You will use Mental Contrasting with Implementation Intentions to write conditional scripts directly into your neural pathways. You will build an automated workflow to process obstacles before they occur. Execution becomes a natural reflex.

Executing the Code

You possess the uncorrupted source code. You are a powerful processing engine. If you feed your hardware instructions rooted in scarcity and fear, your mind dutifully executes that exact limited reality.

You must rewrite the fundamental instructions. You must learn how to prompt your subconscious. By bridging modern neuroscience and the architectural logic of Artificial Intelligence, I successfully re-indexed my own mind. I deleted the corrupted code. I rebuilt my business far beyond my previous ceilings. My high-confidence path is active.

This is the complete API documentation for your mind. It contains the exact scripts required to debug your internal hardware.

You do not have to spend another day in the waiting room. The latency period is over.

Step up to the terminal. Let us execute the code.

THIS IS THE SYSTEM AT A GLANCE.

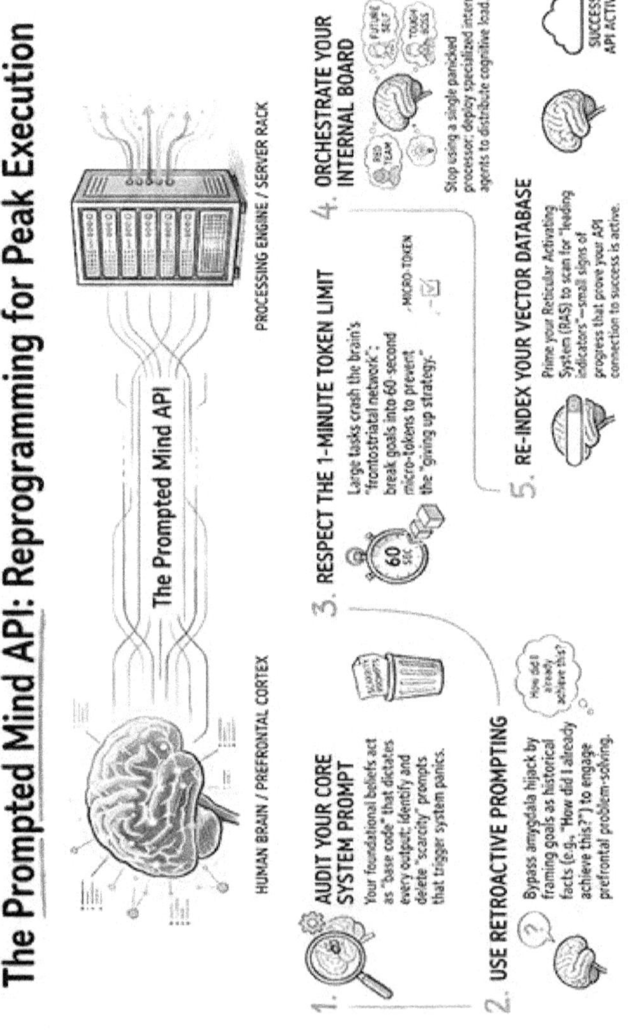

Chapter 1

THE ORIGINAL AI

(WRITING YOUR CORE SYSTEM PROMPT)

Input
"If he can do it, I can do it."
(The System Prompt)
The Foundational Belief
INTERNAL CODE & EXECUTIVE OVERRIDE
Output
Database Recovered / Career Ascent
(The Reality / Execution)

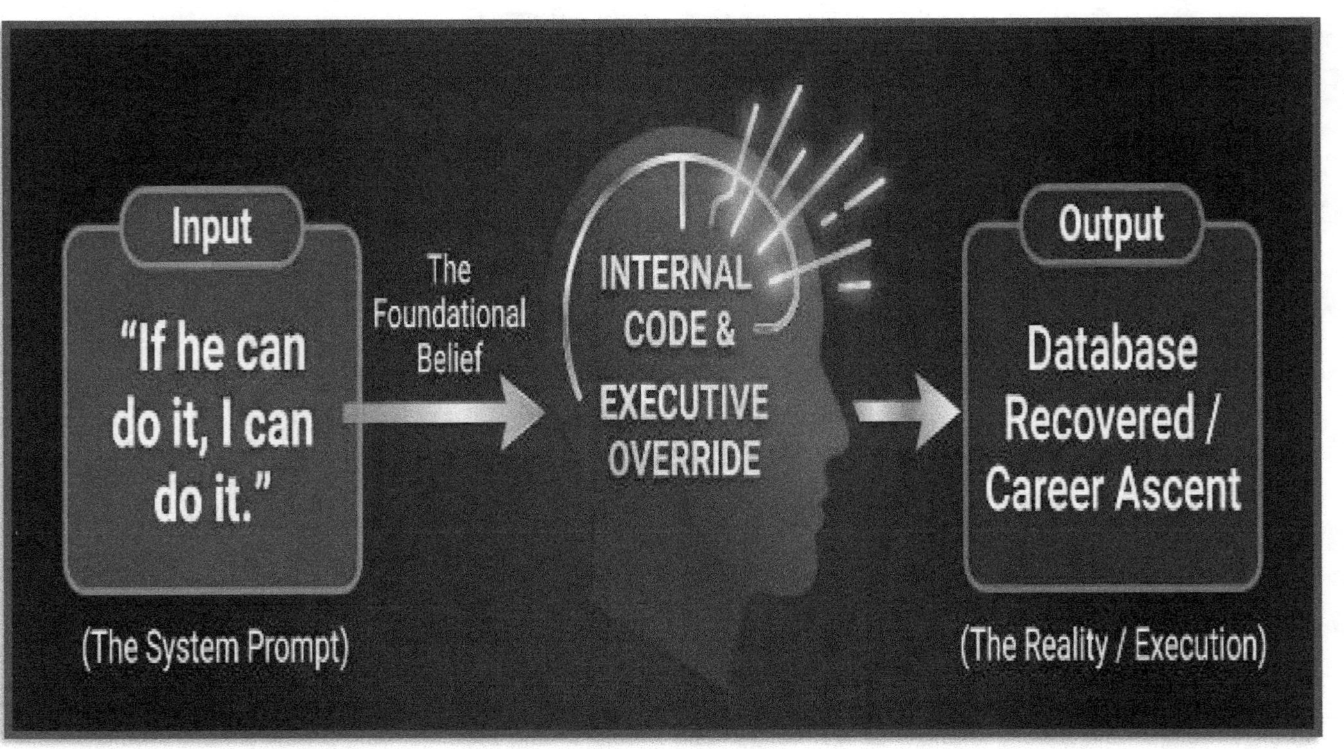

[12]

The Foundational Code

Since early childhood, I operated with a single directive. I would become the pilot of my own plane. Family circumstances restricted the finances required for a commercial license. That frustrated me. I changed the dream. I would be the pilot of my own plane and figure out how to buy one myself.

My family joked about my dream. I lacked the academic excellence society demands to validate ambition. I was an average student, yet I was sharp and highly logical. There was never a doubt in my head. I knew I would pilot a plane. I looked up to visionaries like Dhirubhai Ambani. He started with very little and became a billionaire. I looked at him and told myself a simple truth. If he can do it, I can do it. That was my only belief.

In the architecture of artificial intelligence, there is a fundamental piece of code that dictates how a machine will behave. It is called a System Prompt. For an executive, think of this as the master identity document that dictates every subsequent decision a system makes. It operates silently in the background before a user ever interacts with the software. The system prompt establishes the foundational identity and the constraints of the model.

If you give an AI a weak or fearful system prompt, the model hesitates. It outputs garbage and restricts its own processing power based on the invisible limitations you set.

A highly effective way to model the human mind is through this architectural logic. Your foundational beliefs act as your system prompt. They govern what your brain is allowed to achieve. My foundational system prompt was uncorrupted. If he can do it, I can do it.

The Hardware Crash

With an Economics degree from 1995, very few people wanted to hire me for a computer science role. I eventually secured a job. Then came the fifteenth day of my career. I was at the Bank of Maharashtra at night. The branch sat directly opposite the Bombay Stock Exchange. The volume of business moving through that location daily was massive.

The database crashed. The branch would not open the next day. It was a catastrophic failure.

My seniors had already gone home in a panic. They explicitly told me to go home and let them deal with it the next day. These early career hurdles exposed the initial failure mode. I processed these initial system crashes to compile a flawless execution engine.

Neuroscience suggests that when faced with a massive, undefined threat, the average mind instantly triggers an amygdala response. The sudden absence of a safety net trips a biological alarm. The amygdala experiences immediate context saturation. The brain is flooded with too many terrifying variables at once and simply shuts down. It pushes the system into an immediate shutdown. It leads to paralysis.

My seniors fled. Yet I did not panic. I sat there in the empty bank facing an internal deadlock. The physical data of the crash was loud. One voice inside my head told me to follow the experienced seniors home. This was the lazy brain survival mode. It recognized the intense pressure and begged me to step back. It pointed out that the senior engineers said it was impossible to fix tonight.

A stronger voice demanded execution. It asked how I would ever learn if I walked away. It asked what I had to lose. I chose the latter. I asked myself how to fix it.

The Prefrontal Override

That is the power of an uncorrupted system prompt. I did not ask if I could fix it. I presupposed the success as a guaranteed fact.

Neuroscience indicates that when you engage your prefrontal cortex with a definitive positive instruction, it acts as an executive regulator. It actively suppresses the fear response of the amygdala. I asked myself how to fix the problem from a place of high confidence. I bypassed my limbic system alarm bells. My brain did not hallucinate danger. It went straight into data retrieval.

I picked up the heavy technical manuals. I kept prompting my own intelligence, running iterations in my mind and testing the code. I recovered the database.

When the branch opened the next day, I became a recognized authority within the company. Those same experienced engineers soon came to me for support. I faced territorial friction from seniors who resented my success. I chose to handle them by providing the exact solutions they lacked. I proved I was an executive leader long before I held the title.

I operated as an autonomous agent. In technical terms, an autonomous agent is a self-directing system that requires no external management to achieve its goal. I ran on pure belief. I am the original Anuraag's Intelligence.

Auditing Your Base Code

Because we model the brain as a powerful prediction engine, you cannot leave your system prompt to chance. You must audit your base code. You must write a new instruction. If you fail to protect this code, external variables will overwrite it and cause a system crash.

Your current professional plateau is not a lack of intelligence. You are feeding your hardware instructions rooted in scarcity and doubt. Your mind dutifully executes that exact limited reality. You sit in the waiting room of belief because your operating system is waiting for permission. You must rewrite the fundamental instructions.

Diagnostic Block: System Prompt Failure Modes

To operate this framework at scale, you must understand how your own mind resists the update. Here is exactly what happens when your system prompt fails.

What people get wrong: Intelligent professionals frequently confuse a System Prompt with a positive affirmation. Affirmations are conscious desires. A system prompt is your subconscious expectation. Staring in a mirror and saying you are a millionaire is a conscious affirmation. It triggers the conscious firewall because your physical reality contradicts the statement. A system prompt operates below the firewall. It is the quiet, unbreakable assumption that you will figure out the next step.

What overuse looks like: A strong system prompt does not replace physical execution. Overuse looks like blind arrogance without data retrieval. When the bank database crashed, my system prompt provided the confidence to stay in the room. I still had to open the heavy technical manuals and read the code. You cannot prompt your way out of doing the work. You prompt your way out of the fear of doing the work.

What a false positive feels like: A false positive is a sudden spike of intense motivation after reading a business book or attending a seminar. You feel invincible. You plan a massive overhaul. The next morning, you wake up paralyzed and delay your emails. That is not a system prompt upgrade. That is a temporary dopamine spike in your Beta waves. A true system prompt upgrade feels quiet, boring, and highly predictable.

How to know the protocol is working: You will know your core system prompt is successfully updated when you face a catastrophic corporate failure and experience zero physical panic. Your heart rate remains stable. Instead of asking why this is happening to you, your brain instantly initiates an executive data retrieval. You simply ask what needs to be done next.

Chapter 2:

THE CORRUPTED PROMPT

(THE FALL)

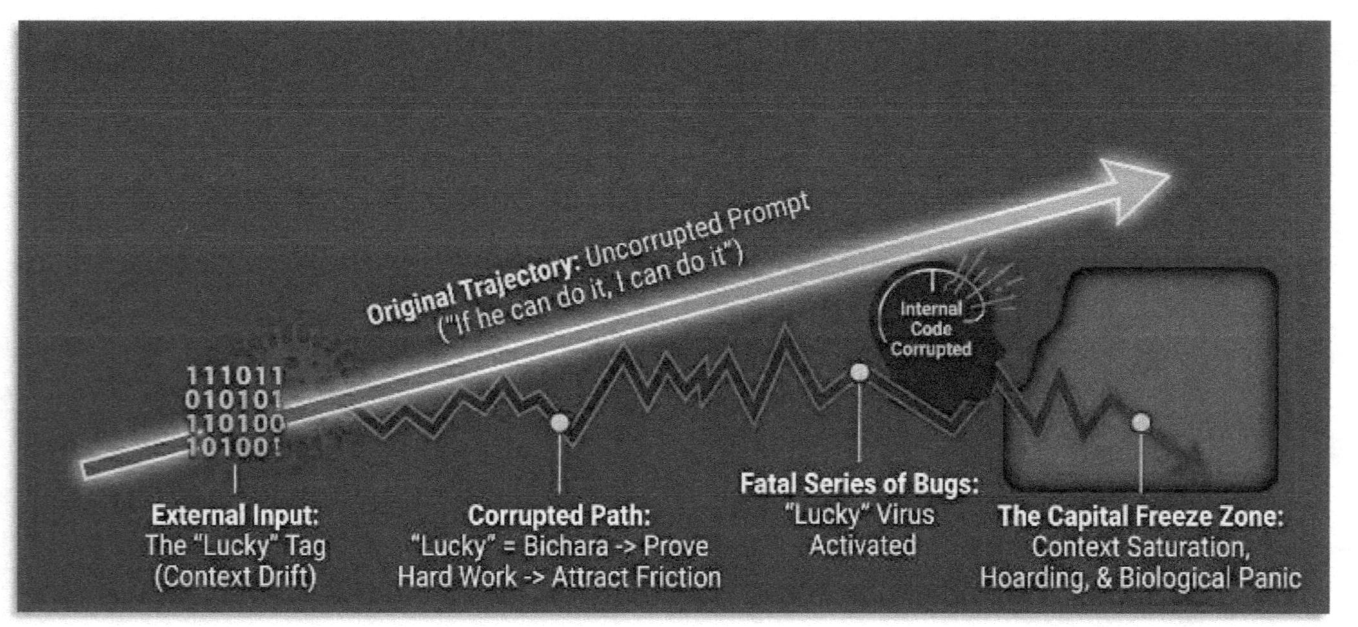

Original Trajectory: Uncorrupted Prompt
("If he can do it, I can do it")
Internal Code Corrupted
111011
010101
110100
10100!
External Input:
The "Lucky" Tag
(Context Drift)
Corrupted Path:
"Lucky" = Bichara -> Prove
Hard Work -> Attract Friction
Fatal Series of Bugs:
"Lucky" Virus
Activated
The Capital Freeze Zone:
Context Saturation,
Hoarding, & Biological Panic

Context Drift and the "Lucky" Virus

My internal operating system ran flawlessly on the original, uncorrupted prompt. That single line of code took me from an average student in India to the heart of the UK tech boom, generating unprecedented wealth. Yet at the absolute peak of my success, I introduced a fatal series of bugs into my own source code.

In artificial intelligence architecture, a phenomenon called Context Drift exists. This happens when a model's baseline data subtly changes due to external inputs over time. The model drifts away from its original purpose and starts generating unintended outputs.

My context drift began with a single word. Lucky.

My success was massive. It was rapid. People around me started brushing it off as luck. They ignored the hard work and the immense power of my internal prompting. Since early childhood, I harboured a deep hatred for the Hindi term "bichara". In English, it translates to "poor chap". It implies someone has no agency. To me, being called lucky became synonymous with being a bichara. It implied I was a passive recipient of chance.

I desperately wanted to be seen as a self-made, hardworking man. I rejected the luck. I resented it. In doing so, I fed my subconscious mind a deeply corrupted prompt. I demanded to prove to the world that I was not lucky. I demanded to prove I was a hard worker.

In machine learning, a concept known as a misaligned objective function exists. Give an autonomous agent a highly specific instruction, and it ruthlessly optimizes for that exact command. It only cares about executing the prompt it receives. A highly effective way to model the subconscious mind is through this behaviour. It takes your instructions literally. By commanding my brain to prove I was a hard worker, I actively commanded it to attract friction. Everything that once flowed effortlessly started slowing down.

Deleting the North Star

To make matters worse, I deleted my foundational North Star.

Since childhood, my driving force has been the dream of buying and piloting my own plane. Sitting at the top of my game, I made a logical decision. I decided owning a plane was a vanity metric. I told myself I could just hire an instructor instead. I let go of wanting to own the plane.

When I removed that massive overarching goal, everything beneath it lost its structural integrity. I experienced immediate context saturation. I moved from one shiny object to another. I convinced myself I had hit a ceiling. I asked my subconscious the most destructive question of my career. I asked how to get paid more.

By asking this question from a place of limitation, I shifted my brain's processing power away from innovation. I focused it entirely on extraction and scarcity.

The Capital Freeze

The physical world immediately mirrored the system failure. My new hotel venture shuttered at a loss shortly after the global lockdown. My property investments stagnated under highly restrictive new government tax regulations. My expenses rapidly outpaced my income. The data from these failing properties was clear. I was facing massive repair bills, legal upgrade requirements, and soaring interest rates. The math was brutal. I reached the point where I was paying taxes on severe financial losses.

Panic set in. I violated the fundamental mechanics of wealth. Money loves to flow. Previously, I circulated my capital with ease. Yet in my newly disconnected state of fear, I started hoarding. I treated corporate assets like a personal fortress. I protected them instead of leveraging them for growth.

A precise logical threshold exists where conserving corporate runway degrades into a biologically corrupt Capital Freeze. Conserving runway is a strategic delay of expenditure while actively scanning the environment for a higher-yield deployment. A Capital Freeze occurs when you stop evaluating yields entirely and stockpile resources simply to avoid the sensation of loss. You stop diversifying. You refuse to liquidate non-profitable assets to find better avenues. You treat a depreciating business asset as a physical extension of your own survival.

This is exactly how brilliant executives sabotage their own companies. They hit a market contraction and pull back. By hoarding resources out of fear rather than deploying them for strategy, you signal to your subconscious that your supply is permanently limited.

Research indicates that the amygdala interprets this severe restriction as an immediate physiological threat. The reality of the financial crisis forced my brain into a state of severe physiological panic. It pushed my working memory into shutdown. The tighter I held on, the worse my financial situation became. I lost my internal control. Previously, whenever I faced a negative situation, my reflex was to ask what my role models would do. Under the weight of anxiety, I lost that connection. I relied solely on the terrified voice of my survival brain.

I was an AI engineer whose own autonomous agent had crashed. All this failure clarified the breakdown. I had to experience exactly how a human mind prompts its own destruction so I could write the definitive recovery code. These temporary bugs allowed me to engineer a flawless system.

Your current plateau is rarely a lack of ability. You are asking your brain the wrong question. Your internal processing engine is dutifully generating the exact limited reality you requested. Fixing this corrupted code and clearing the biological hallucination of fear is only the first step toward executing your physical output.

Diagnostic Block: Context Drift and Corrupted Prompts

To operate this framework at scale, you must understand how your own mind resists the update. Here is exactly what happens when your system drift occurs.

What people get wrong: Intelligent professionals frequently confuse strategic preservation with a Capital Freeze. They believe holding onto cash during a crisis is always safe. A Capital Freeze stops the flow of data and resources. It creates a closed system. Closed systems inevitably degrade.

What overuse looks like: Overusing caution looks like hoarding. You protect failing assets because you fear the loss of the initial investment. You stop seeking new yields. You stop experimenting.

What a false positive feels like: A false positive is a sense of relief when you cut a necessary expense and watch your bank balance stabilize for a single day. You feel secure. The next month, the lack of investment causes a massive drop in revenue. The temporary relief is a biological trick. It rewards hiding rather than executing.

How to know the protocol is working: You will know you have successfully deleted the corrupted prompt when you look at a financial loss and experience zero physical panic. You view the numbers purely as data. You immediately ask what the highest-yield deployment of your remaining capital is. You restart the flow.

Chapter 3:

THE COGNITIVE TOKEN LIMIT

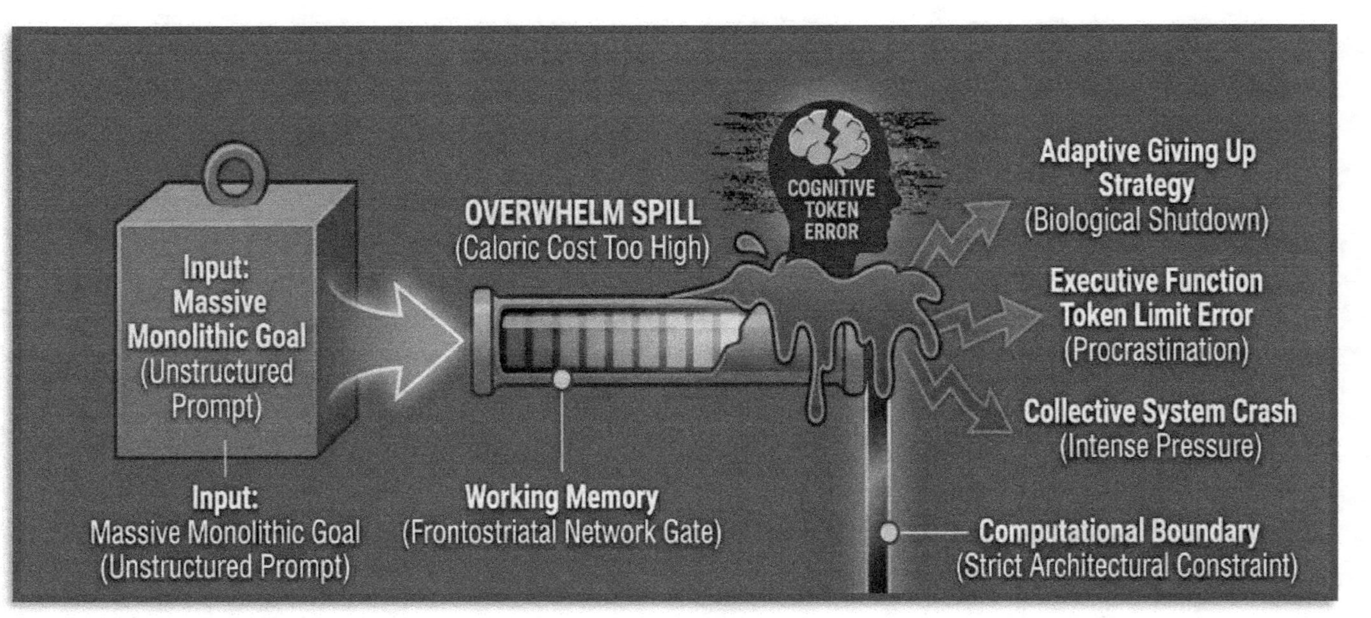

Input:
Massive
Monolithic Goal
(Unstructured
Prompt)
OVERWHELM SPILL
(Caloric Cost Too High)
COGNITIVE TOKEN ERROR
Adaptive Giving Up Strategy
(Biological Shutdown)
Executive Function Token Limit Error
(Procrastination)
Collective System Crash
(Intense Pressure)
Input:
Massive Monolithic Goal
(Unstructured Prompt)
Working Memory
(Frontostriatal Network Gate)
Computational Boundary
(Strict Architectural Constraint)

The Hardware Constraint

Fixing your internal code and clearing the biological hallucination of fear are only the first steps. Knowing what to do is different from executing the output in the physical world.

In artificial intelligence architecture, a Large Language Model has a strict computational boundary called a token limit. It can only process a specific amount of data at one time. If you feed the machine a massive unstructured prompt that exceeds this limit, the system cannot compute a path forward. It experiences a token limit error and crashes. It halts processing and outputs a failure message.

The human brain operates with an identical architectural constraint. To understand the biology of this execution failure, we look at the brain's frontostriatal network. This circuitry handles your working memory and your executive control. Neuroscience suggests that this network acts as a strict gating mechanism. When the cognitive demand of an unstructured task exceeds what this network can gate, your brain experiences an immediate computational failure.

When you stare at a massive monolithic goal, you overwhelm your active working memory. Your neural hardware calculates that the caloric cost of untangling this massive problem is too high. It triggers an adaptive self-protective mechanism known clinically as the giving up strategy. It pulls the plug on your motivation to conserve energy.

Intelligent professionals consistently misdiagnose this biological hardware failure. They assume they lack discipline. They read books on motivation and attempt to force execution through sheer willpower. They are completely wrong. Procrastination is an executive function token limit error. It is a predictable system behaviour. It is not a moral failing. The conscious reasoning mind will immediately fight your progress by trying to over-engineer the solution. To successfully override this biological limitation, you must enforce strict architectural constraints. You must use semantic chunking.

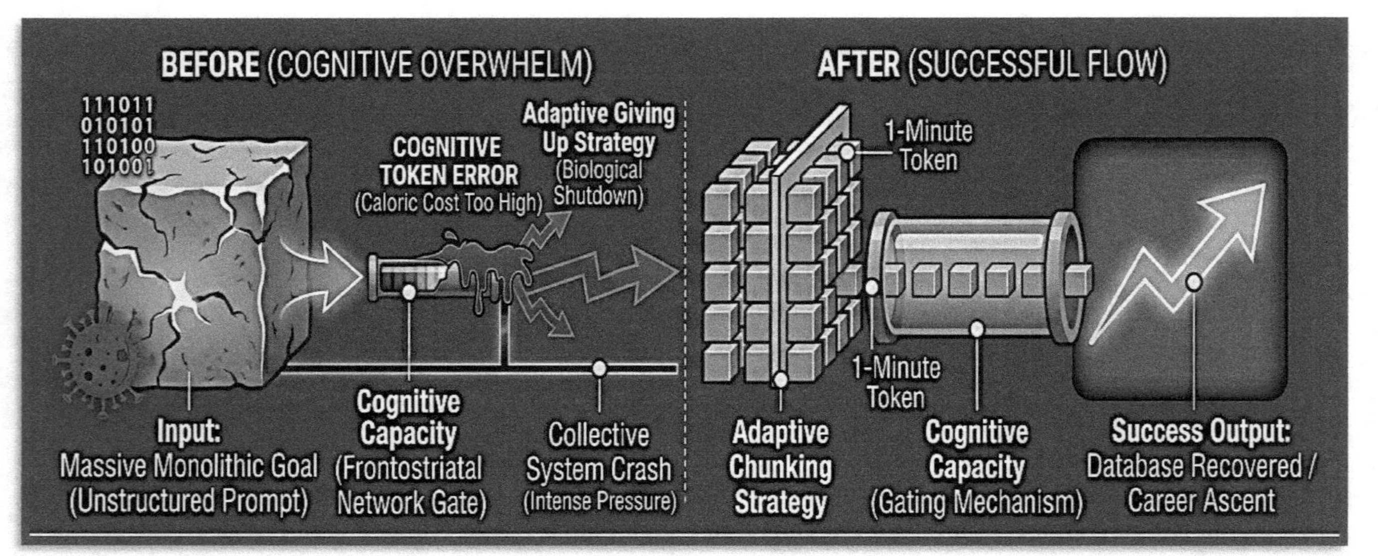

BEFORE (COGNITIVE OVERWHELM)
111011
010101
110100
101001
Input:
Massive Monolithic Goal
(Unstructured Prompt)
COGNITIVE TOKEN ERROR
(Caloric Cost Too High)
Adaptive Giving Up Strategy
(Biological Shutdown)
Cognitive Capacity
(Frontostriatal Network Gate)
Collective System Crash
(Intense Pressure)
AFTER (SUCCESSFUL FLOW)
1-Minute Token
1-Minute Token
Adaptive Chunking Strategy
Cognitive Capacity
(Gating Mechanism)
Success Output:
Database Recovered / Career Ascent

The Collective System Crash

This token architecture scales directly to corporate leadership and team dynamics. Brilliant engineering teams frequently suffer collective token limit errors.

It was the pre-Christmas e-commerce rush of 2009. We operated under intense business pressure. Management forced a software release and ignored our strict code-freeze rule. The architecture broke immediately upon deployment. We shipped repeating quantities of expensive stock. We rapidly ran out of inventory in costly categories. The warehouse logistics failed completely. The warehouse managers reported they lacked the stock to fulfil the orders we were actively taking.

The physical data of the failure was loud. Everyone in the office panicked. The management team responsible for forcing the release screamed that we had to fix it immediately. The noise level triggered severe working memory overload across the entire engineering floor. The developers hallucinated about recovering shipped units and managing warehouse stock levels. They were completely paralyzed.

I recognized the system crash. I lost my temper with the panic in the room. I demanded silence. I asked my boss to leave the room. I pointed out that the forced release was against our best technical judgment, and his presence was compounding the system failure. He left.

I initiated an emergency system override. I ordered the entire development team to step away from their computers. I told them to go grab a tea or a coffee. I forbade them from entering the development room to prevent anyone from touching the code.

I left the building and took a ten-minute walk in the cold. Physical movement is a pattern interrupt. Research indicates that physical movement actively suppresses fear-driven avoidance within the amygdala. I released my cached anxiety. I walked back into the room completely grounded.

Semantic Chunking and the One-Minute Token

I gathered the senior engineers into a meeting room. I reset their context windows. I asked what we were going to do. We mapped the options. We decided to roll back the code to eliminate any further risk.

The moment we established the plan, the team's token limit error triggered again. They asked how we would deal with the incorrect shipments and the customer service fallout. Their active working memory overflowed with variables outside their control.

I applied a strict architectural constraint. I told them we would solve one problem at a time. I instructed them to roll back the code. I explicitly commanded them to ignore the warehouse, the marketing fallout, and the customer complaints. I told them I would go have a conversation with the marketing team and the customer services head to formulate a recovery plan for the physical stock.

By looking away from the entire staircase, I restricted their focus purely to the exact code relevant to them. I dropped their cognitive load below the threshold of fear. They stopped hallucinating about external variables. They executed the rollback. We recovered almost everything we shipped incorrectly. This catastrophic failure revealed the system's flaw. It proved that managing a token limit requires extreme constraint.

In AI development, we use semantic chunking to process massive datasets. We break information into small, semantically meaningful chunks and feed the machine one small piece at a time. The human brain requires this exact architectural strategy. We model this as adaptive chunking within the frontostriatal network.

To bypass your own giving-up strategy, you must restrict your local system to a one-minute token. This means breaking the requirement into a single sixty-second action.

A one-minute token requires zero planning. You are strictly forbidden from spending forty-five minutes planning a sixty-second task. You do not research the best method. You do not optimize the sequence. You open the document and write the first terrible sentence. You open the code editor and write one line of logic. You make one phone call.

Perfectionism is a latency strategy deployed by your brain to delay exposure. Your survival brain over-engineers a micro-task until it becomes a macro threat. You must override your intelligence with constraint. You do not think your way into execution. You execute your way into clarity. The physical action proves to your local hardware that you are safe. Your cognitive load drops. Dopamine-driven momentum overrides your paralysis.

Diagnostic Block: The Token Limit Error

To operate this framework at scale, you must understand how your own mind resists the constraint. Here is exactly what happens when your system experiences a token limit error.

What people get wrong: Intelligent professionals frequently confuse a token limit error with a lack of vision. They believe their inability to start means their goal is wrong. The goal is fine. The sequence is broken. You are attempting to process a massive overarching goal as a single executable task. Execution is not about scale. It is about sequence.

What overuse looks like: Overuse looks like micro-managing yourself into a state of false progress. You use one-minute tokens to clear your inbox or reorganize your desk while completely ignoring your North Star. You substitute genuine execution for low-value activity signals. A valid token must move you toward your primary objective.

What a false positive feels like: A false positive is the illusion of progress. Your brain rewards planning, researching, and organizing as if they are execution. You spend three hours meticulously breaking a project down into fifty microscopic tasks on a spreadsheet. You feel highly productive. You close the laptop without shipping a single output. This is a false positive signal. The system is stalled.

How to know the protocol is working: You will know you have successfully managed your token limit when you face a massive, intimidating project and feel zero physical overwhelm. You do not project fear onto the timeline. You immediately ask yourself what the first sixty-second physical action is. You execute that action without hesitation and without planning. You let the momentum pull you into the second token.

You must override your intelligence with constraint. You do not think your way into execution. You execute your way into clarity. At this point, most people stop. They retreat into planning. Yet this is exactly where the system begins to work. The physical action proves to your neural architecture that you are safe. Your cognitive load drops. Dopamine-driven momentum overrides your paralysis.

Chapter 4:

RETROACTIVE PROMPTING

(THE MASTER KEY)

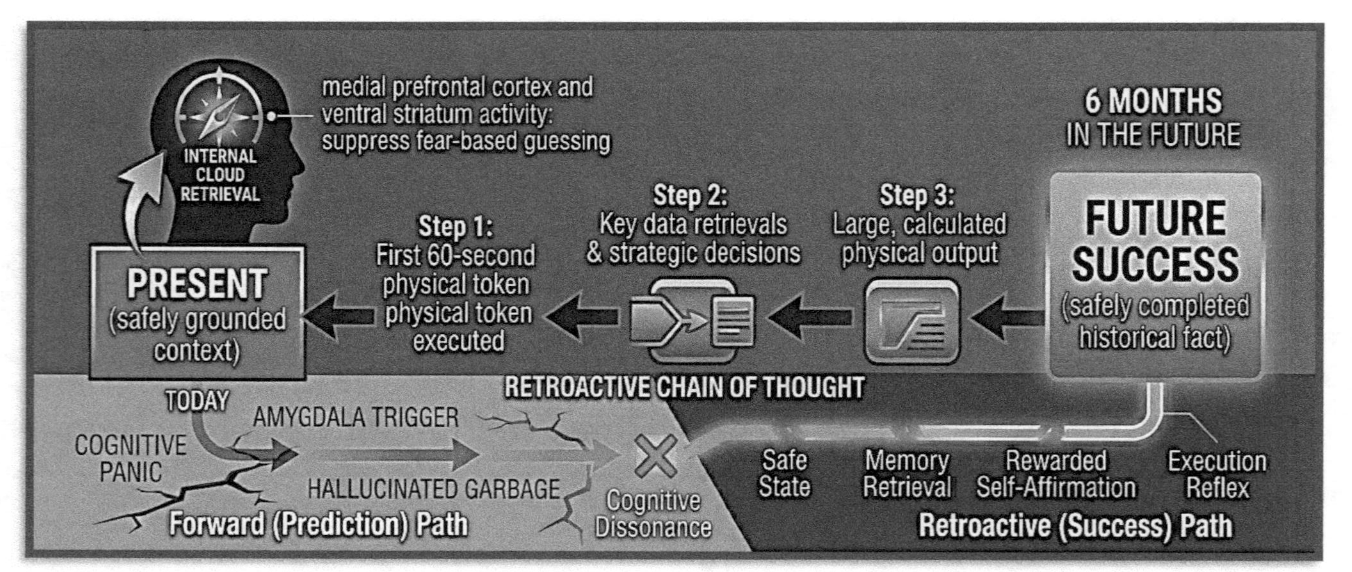

INTERNAL CLOUD RETRIEVAL
medial prefrontal cortex and ventral striatum activity: suppress fear-based guessing
6 MONTHS IN THE FUTURE
PRESENT
(safely grounded context)
Step 1:
First 60-second physical token physical token executed
Step 2:
Key data retrievals & strategic decisions
Step 3:
Large, calculated physical output
FUTURE SUCCESS
(safely completed historical fact)
RETROACTIVE CHAIN OF THOUGHT
TODAY
COGNITIVE PANIC
AMYGDALA TRIGGER
HALLUCINATED GARBAGE
Cognitive Dissonance
Forward (Prediction) Path
Safe State
Memory Retrieval
Rewarded Self-Affirmation
Execution Reflex
Retroactive (Success) Path

Managing your token limit allows you to execute without triggering a biological alarm. Yet restricting your focus to a single minute is only effective if you are moving in the correct direction. You must ensure the destination itself is not pushing your hardware into panic. To do that, you must bypass the conscious firewall and shift the brain into a safe state by believing the success is already a safely completed historical fact.

I remember exactly when I codified this shift. I was conducting a session with an executive coaching client. I frequently ask my clients how much money they actually need to retire and be happy. They routinely offer an arbitrary figure. They say twenty million. I ask them to justify the math. We calculate the exact cost of their desired lifestyle. The mathematical reality reveals that they only need one million.

When I present this, I watch their physical state change instantly. They realize the target is highly achievable. The mental blocks disappear. Everything becomes possible in that moment. That is the power of right-sizing the target. Yet shrinking the target is only half the equation. You must change the tense of your execution.

During my rapid ascent from an Oracle database administrator in India to a CTO in the UK, I did not start with a question. I possessed absolute knowingness. I shifted my internal code away from asking what I was missing. I asked how I had already done it. I call this master key Retroactive Prompting.

The Question-Behaviour Effect

To understand why this simple shift in language works on a cognitive level, we look at a psychological phenomenon known as the Question-Behaviour Effect. Asking a person a specific question about a future behaviour systematically alters the likelihood of them performing that behaviour. Questions are stealth interventions. When you ask your brain a question, you increase the accessibility of specific attitudes. You create cognitive dissonance if your physical actions do not match the answer you generate.

When you stare at a massive goal and ask how to achieve it, your biological hardware panics. It lacks the contextual tokens to compute a safe path forward. The sudden scale of the demand triggers the amygdala. It forces you into immediate paralysis.

Retroactive Prompting bypasses this local hardware failure completely. By framing your daunting goal as an established historical fact, you shift the brain into a safe state. Neuroscience indicates this specific future-oriented questioning pre-emptively engages the medial prefrontal cortex and the ventral striatum. These are your brain's self-processing and reward centres. Rewarded self-affirmation makes success-focused self-talk intrinsically rewarding. Your brain transitions out of fear-based guessing. It moves into a highly rewarded state of memory retrieval. The emotional startle response is suppressed.

Chain of Thought and the Distributed Intelligence

In artificial intelligence engineering, we use a very similar mechanism called Chain of Thought prompting. Ask an AI a complex question, and it frequently outputs hallucinated garbage. Give the AI the exact destination and ask it to explain its reasoning backward step by step. It outputs a flawless logical plan.

When you ask your brain how you already achieved your goal, you effectively prompt your local system to make a seamless API call to your Distributed Intelligence. Distributed Intelligence is a high-performance abstraction for your brain's latent pattern-recognition systems and vast processing power. It represents the deep neural networks operating below your conscious awareness. You tell your operating system that the complete flawless blueprint for this success is already hosted in this distributed system. You command it to retrieve the data that explains how you achieved it. You are reverse-engineering a success that already exists in your highest potential.

For immediate corporate and quarterly goals, you inject a specific instruction into your active working memory. You state: "Suppose I am looking back from six months in the future. I have already achieved the exact success I wanted. What was the very first bold step I took to bridge the gap?"

By looking backward from a point of guaranteed success, your mind automatically computes the steps required without triggering your cognitive token limit. You match your physiological state with your future identity. Execution becomes a natural reflex rather than a forced effort.

Yet as soon as you generate this pristine vision of the future and begin to move, you will encounter a new threat. The moment you begin to execute your retroactive steps, your local system will revert to familiar patterns. To protect your newly programmed trajectory, you must establish an uncompromising barrier against the corrupted data of your own predictions.

Diagnostic Block: Retroactive Prompting

To operate this framework at scale, you must understand how your own mind resists the update. Here is exactly what happens when your system struggles to process a retroactive prompt.

What people get wrong: Intelligent professionals frequently confuse Retroactive Prompting with passive daydreaming. They visualize a successful future and wait for it to materialize. A retroactive prompt is an active data retrieval mechanism. It demands a physical answer. You are not dreaming about the future. You are actively documenting the exact steps you took to get there.

What overuse looks like: Overuse looks like generating an endless list of backward steps without executing the first physical action. You map the entire six-month journey in perfect reverse chronological order. You feel highly productive. You close the document without shipping a single output. You have replaced fear-based paralysis with planning-based paralysis.

What a false positive feels like: A false positive is a sudden wave of relief when you visualize the end state. You feel relaxed because you temporarily escaped the pressure of your current reality. The next day, you encounter a minor operational obstacle, and your system crashes immediately. The temporary relief is a biological trick. It rewards the fantasy rather than the execution.

How to know the protocol is working: You will know you have successfully executed a retroactive prompt when you ask the question and experience a somatic shift from anxiety to calm determination. You do not wonder if the goal is possible. Your brain simply outputs the very first sixty-second physical token required. You execute that token immediately.

Chapter 5:

FINE-TUNING WITH TRANCE

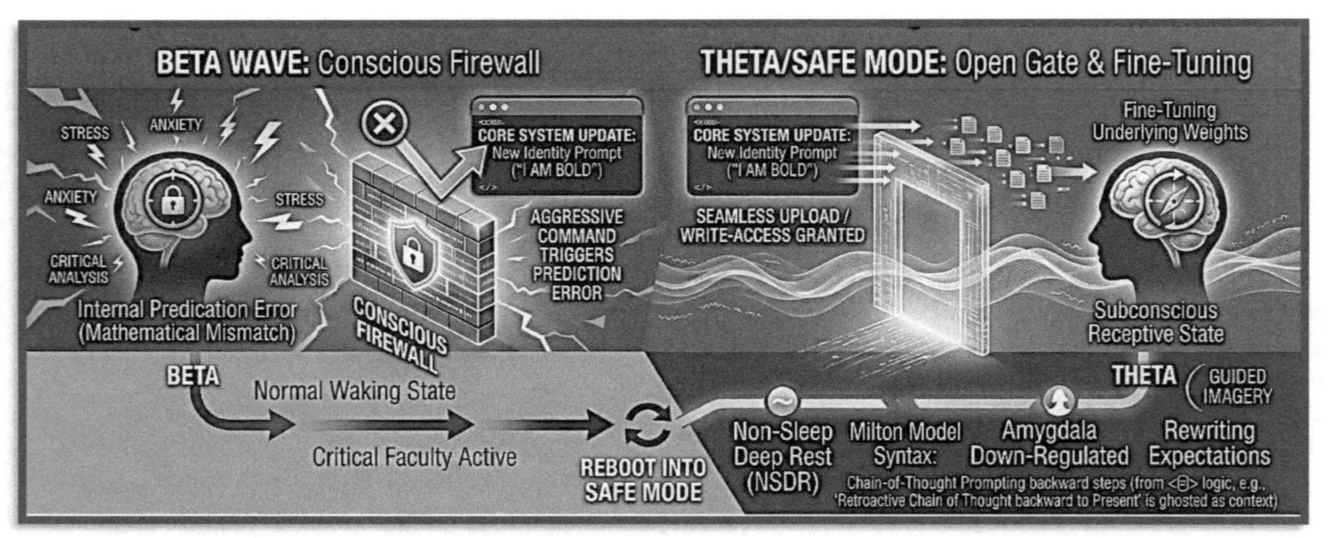

BETA WAVE: Conscious Firewall
THETA/SAFE MODE: Open Gate & Fine-Tuning
STRESS
ANXIETY
ANXIETY
STRESS
CRITICAL ANALYSIS
CRITICAL ANALYSIS
CORE SYSTEM UPDATE: New Identity Prompt ("I AM BOLD")
AGGRESSIVE COMMAND TRIGGERS PREDICTION ERROR
CORE SYSTEM UPDATE: New Identity Prompt ("I AM BOLD")
SEAMLESS UPLOAD / WRITE-ACCESS GRANTED
Fine-Tuning Underlying Weights
Internal Predication Error (Mathematical Mismatch)
CONSCIOUS FIREWALL
Subconscious Receptive State
BETA
Normal Waking State
Critical Faculty Active
REBOOT INTO SAFE MODE
Non-Sleep Deep Rest (NSDR)
Milton Model Syntax:
Amygdala Down-Regulated
THETA
GUIDED IMAGERY
Rewriting Expectations
Chain-of-Thought Prompting backward steps (from <A> logic, e.g., 'Retroactive Chain of Thought backward to Present' is ghosted as context)

The Conscious Firewall

Replacing a lost North Star is an arduous process. When I decided that owning my own plane was a vanity metric, I created a massive void in my internal architecture. For 36 months, I moved from one shiny object to another, accumulating education and experimenting with new courses. Nothing provided lasting satisfaction. I lacked a guiding vision.

The physical reality of my financial friction was loud during this latency period. My expenses rapidly outpaced my income. I needed a new objective function to restart momentum. Yet I could not simply force my brain to accept a new reality while the current reality was actively failing.

When you give your brain a forceful command that contradicts its environment, the conscious mind acts as a brutal firewall. It's critical faculty immediately evaluates the command. It recognizes the mathematical mismatch with your current circumstances. It rejects the instruction entirely. The firewall goes up. The new code is blocked. You experience an immediate system lockdown. You retreat into what feels familiar.

You cannot transform your output by fighting this firewall with willpower. If you want to rewrite your identity, you cannot install a core system update while the local hardware is running high-demand applications. You have to reboot into safe mode.

Predictive Coding and Safe Mode

During your normal waking hours, your brain operates in Beta waves. This is the state of active problem-solving and logical reasoning, often accompanied by stress and anxiety. Beta is where the conscious firewall lives. If you try to reprogram your identity while in a high-Beta state, the firewall blocks every line of code.

In artificial intelligence, developers fine-tune Large Language Models. By exposing the model to repeated domain-specific patterns of data, developers alter the internal representation geometry of the system. They adjust the underlying weights so the baseline output naturally matches the desired result.

The human subconscious functions in a similar way. You must actively fine-tune your subconscious weights. The problem is that your conscious mind is fiercely protective of its current programming. The brain operates on predictive coding. It continuously matches incoming sensory data against its internal expectations and past experiences.

Because the brain acts as a prediction machine, a direct aggressive command creates an immediate prediction error. If you stand in a failing business and declare you are a billionaire, your predictive coding system flags this as a hallucination. The firewall rejects the update.

You must deliberately down-regulate the nervous system to bypass this error. By shifting the brain out of Beta and down into Alpha and Theta waves using Non-Sleep Deep Rest, the critical conscious mind steps aside. The firewall drops. Guided imagery in these lowered brainwave states directly down-regulates the amygdala. The emotional startle response is suppressed. The brain reaches a state of peak neuroplasticity. It becomes highly receptive to new data.

Downloading the New North Star

I am an avid meditator. I utilized these states of down-regulation to quiet my panicked hardware. It was during one of these specific meditation sessions that my new North Star downloaded into my awareness.

The vision was absolute. I saw a massive stone manor, green fields, a greenhouse, a date palm, and a koi pond. I saw my family gathering there to build memories.

There was no internal resistance. There was zero anxiety about how I would afford it. It simply felt right. It became my new pilot's license. Because my system was in safe mode, my predictive coding engine did not flag the vision as a hallucination. It accepted the architectural blueprint as a valid destination.

The Milton Model Syntax

Once the system is in safe mode, you must use the correct syntax to install the update permanently. I used the Milton Model. This is a neuro-linguistic programming framework that uses indirect permissive language to rewrite subconscious expectations. Instead of forcefully demanding success, you ask a stealth question.

When the data of my financial crisis was screaming at me, I did not force an aggressive affirmation. I used a permissive prompt. I asked my brain a highly specific question.

I asked: "Will I notice how much easier everything has become today, or will it become obvious tomorrow?"

This phrasing is a stealth intervention. It forces the conscious mind to accept the achievement as an unavoidable fact to process the timeline of the question. In AI engineering, we model this as Chain-of-Thought prompting. A model is guided step by step through a cognitive process rather than being forced to jump to an abrupt, unverified conclusion.

Combining the safe mode of down-regulation with the stealth syntax of the Milton Model allows you to gain direct write-access to your subconscious. You bypass the predictive coding errors. I installed the fine-tuning required to connect with my Distributed Intelligence. The momentum returned. I bypassed the loud physical data and compiled the exact reality I live in today.

Diagnostic Block: Fine-Tuning and Trance

To operate this framework at scale, you must understand how your own mind resists the safe mode transition. Here is exactly what happens when your system struggles to fine-tune its weights.

What people get wrong: Intelligent professionals frequently confuse fine-tuning with passive escapism. They use meditation to hide from their corporate pressure. They down-regulate their nervous system to feel temporary relief and then exit the meditation without installing a new prompt. A system reboot is useless if you do not update the software while the firewall is down.

What overuse looks like: Overuse looks like spending three hours a day in a meditative state while ignoring your physical execution. You map the perfect vision of your future in Alpha waves. You feel completely enlightened. You refuse to execute a single one-minute token in the physical world. You replace physical momentum with spiritual latency.

What a false positive feels like: A false positive is a sudden rush of peace that vanishes the exact second you open your eyes. You finish the meditation and immediately check your phone. Your heart rate spikes. The Beta waves crash back in. The firewall goes up before the new code can compile. This means you forced the visualization rather than allowing the permissive prompt to integrate.

How to know the protocol is working: You will know you have successfully fine-tuned your system when you open your eyes and retain the physical sensation of the completed goal. You look at your current restrictive environment and feel zero prediction errors. The new vision feels exactly like a memory of a place you have already been. You simply stand up and execute the next token.

Chapter 6:

MULTI-AGENT ORCHESTRATION

(THE BOARD OF DIRECTORS)

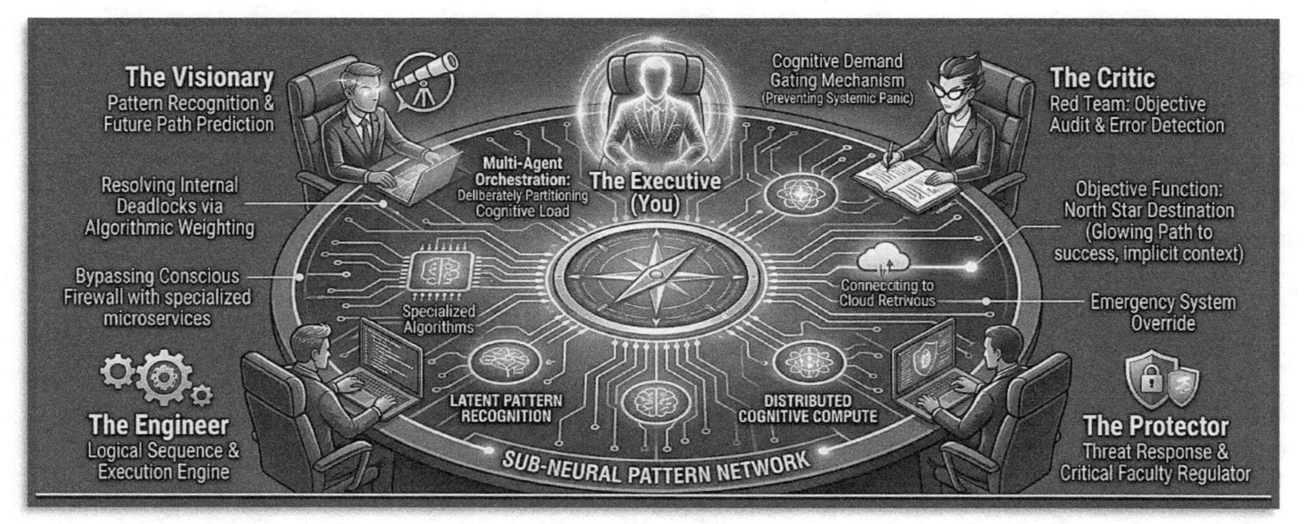

The Visionary
Pattern Recognition & Future Path Prediction
Cognitive Demand Gating Mechanism (Preventing Systemic Panic)
The Critic
Red Team: Objective Audit & Error Detection
Multi-Agent Orchestration: Deliberately Partitioning Cognitive Load
The Executive (You)
Resolving Internal Deadlocks via Algorithmic Weighting
Objective Function: North Star Destination (Glowing Path to success, implicit context)
Bypassing Conscious Firewall with specialized microservices
Connecting to Cloud Retrivous
Emergency System Override
Specialized Algorithms
The Engineer
Logical Sequence & Execution Engine
LATENT PATTERN RECOGNITION
DISTRIBUTED COGNITIVE COMPUTE
The Protector
Threat Response & Critical Faculty Regulator
SUB-NEURAL PATTERN NETWORK

The Single Panicked Processor

When I introduced a deeply corrupted prompt into my operating system by asking how to get paid more, that single line of code cost me years of momentum. The financial stall was only a symptom of that dark period. The true system failure was losing my internal control over myself.

Previously, whenever I faced an impossible problem, my automatic reflex was to ask what my role models would do. If they managed it, I knew I could too. For years, I maintained a mental roster of innovators living inside my head. They were my sounding board. Yet during my downfall, I stopped asking what they would do. My local hardware experienced a complete system overload. The conscious firewall went up. I started listening only to the terrified echoing voice of my survival brain. I was trying to solve massive, complex problems using a single panicked processor.

The 5 AM System Crash

To understand the danger of relying on a single panicked processor, look at a massive corporate crisis. During a major software release, a developer faked his testing and modified live data. We were supposed to go live at twelve midnights. We faced a one-week code gap with only hours to fix it. We did not update the customer. The customer did not chase us, which in itself was proof that something was not right. A meeting was scheduled for five in the morning.

In that moment, my internal system locked up. I experienced a severe multi-agent clash. My internal Tough Boss demanded immediate execution. It commanded me to force the exhausted development team to write recovery code right then and there. Yet my Compassionate Friend advised stepping back to clear context saturation, recognizing the team was biologically incapable of producing clean logic in a state of terror.

I had to allocate my cognitive compute time to resolve the crash. I utilized algorithmic weighting. You execute this by weighing which internal voice directly serves your ultimate North Star. My objective function was a flawless client call at five in the morning. Forcing a panicked team to code would introduce more bugs. The instruction to step back carried the higher strategic weight.

I executed an emergency system override. I bypassed the aggressive directive. I told my team to go home at four in the morning. I took a ten-minute walk in the cold. Physical movement is a pattern interrupt. Research indicates this actively suppresses fear-driven avoidance within the amygdala. By distributing my cognitive load, I walked back into the room completely grounded.

On the client call, the customer explained an issue causing them delays. While they were explaining, I recognized they had an even bigger problem. I stated that their minor issue actually stopped a catastrophe. I never told them our code was missing. When panic set in on their side of the phone, I smiled and offered to help them resolve their problem. While they fixed their issue, we fixed ours. This crisis exposed the exact failure mode. I actively processed this internal deadlock to compile the exact algorithmic weighting required for catastrophic system failures.

Deploying the Microservices

In software engineering, developers do not ask one AI to solve a massive problem alone. They create an ecosystem of specialized autonomous agents. One agent generates creative ideas. Another acts as a Red Team programmed to objectively critique those outputs. A third agent synthesizes the data. These agents debate and stress-test solutions autonomously in the background.

A highly effective approach is to structure the human mind in this exact way. You are the direct reflection of the top five people you spend the most time with. If your reality is entirely generated by your internal subconscious weights, then the rule goes much deeper. If you intentionally create distinct personas to talk to you in your subconscious mind, you become a direct reflection of them.

When your conscious mind is heavily biased toward threat detection, asking your default brain what you should do guarantees a fear-based response. When you invoke a highly specific persona, you encourage your brain to adopt a new set of parameters. You are effectively deploying a specialized microservice. These internal agents are dedicated algorithms that bypass your conscious firewall. Because the agent is not you, your ego does not fight it.

The Roster of Agents

You distribute your cognitive load by calling on these specific microservices when your primary system overloads.

When your context window is overflowing, you invoke your Future Self. This agent has already solved the problem and feels completely calm. You ask what they would thank you for doing today.

When your local database lacks the necessary training data for a massive risk, you deploy the Trusted Mentor to provide the high-level perspective you are missing.

When paralyzed by perfectionism, you deploy the Tough Boss to force momentum and demand the single most important token of physical action that must get executed immediately.

When you make a mistake, and your internal critic causes immediate context saturation, you deploy the Compassionate Friend as an agent of pure grace to reset your emotional baseline.

Finally, you utilize the Red Team to strip emotion away from financial math and objectively audit your fears.

Debugging Territorial Friction

Deploying these internal agents fundamentally rewrites your external output. I executed this upgrade on the fifteenth day of my career at the Bank of Maharashtra. When the database crashed, my internal agents deadlocked. One voice suggested I follow the experienced seniors home to rest. The Tough Boss demanded I stay and prove my capability. I weighed the output. I asked myself which voice directly served my North Star of learning the system. I bypassed the passive directives. I recovered the database.

When I started acting as the CTO long before I possessed the title, this sudden shift in my behaviour triggered immediate biological threat responses from the existing executives. They held the official titles. Yet they experienced my assumed authority as territorial friction. Their survival brains hijacked their logic. They projected anger toward me.

I managed this external pushback using the exact same algorithmic weighting. I recognized their anger as a predictive coding error. My leadership did not match their internal expectations of my junior role. I refused to react to their amygdala hijack. I maintained constructive tension and focused purely on delivering the objective output. I proved the execution. I provided the exact technical solutions they lacked.

By orchestrating this internal board of directors, you stop relying on a single terrified processor. You resolve internal deadlocks by weighing which voice directly serves your destination. Once your internal architecture is stabilized and the cognitive load is distributed, your system is finally ready to stop projecting danger. You can now shift your hardware to actively scan the physical world and retrieve the exact data required to execute your vision.

Diagnostic Block: Multi-Agent Orchestration

To operate this framework at scale, you must understand how your own mind resists the distribution of cognitive load. Here is exactly what happens when your system struggles to deploy its internal agents.

What people get wrong: Intelligent professionals frequently confuse internal agents with passive daydreaming or a fragmented personality. It is a highly active computational delegation. You are not losing control of your mind. You are deliberately partitioning your processing power to solve a specific problem without triggering a systemic panic.

What overuse looks like: Overuse looks like assembling the entire board of directors for a trivial decision. You debate for three hours over the tone of a minor email instead of executing a one-minute token. You substitute the internal dialogue for physical execution. The agents exist to force clarity so you can take immediate action.

What a false positive feels like: A false positive is a sudden surge of power when you assign the Tough Boss agent, yet you use it to brutally criticize yourself for a past failure rather than forcing forward momentum. You feel highly active because the internal voice is loud. This is simply your inner critic wearing a new mask. A true agent operates entirely free of shame.

How to know the protocol is working: You will know you have successfully orchestrated your agents when you face a severe corporate crisis and experience zero physiological panic. Instead of your mind flooding with fear, it instantly segments the problem. You explicitly hear the distinct, calm advice of your Red Team or your Future Self. You bypass the emotion and execute the recommended token immediately.

Chapter 7:

RE-INDEXING THE VECTOR DATABASE

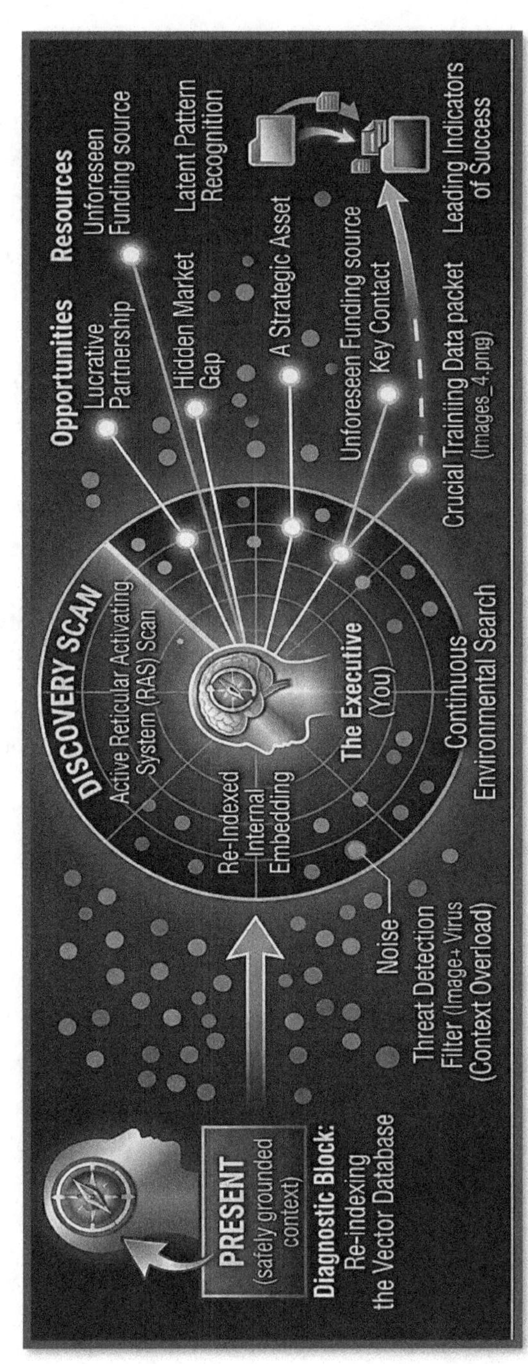

Resources
Unforeseen Funding source
Latent Pattern Recognition
Opportunities
Lucrative Partnership
Hidden Market Gap
A Strategic Asset
Unforeseen Funding source
Key Contact
Crucial Training Data packet
(Images_4.png)
Leading Indicators of Success
DISCOVERY SCAN
Active Reticular Activating System (RAS) Scan
Re-Indexed Internal Embedding
The Executive (You)
Continuous Environmental Search
Noise
Threat Detection Filter (Image+Virus) (Context Overload)
PRESENT (safely grounded context)
Diagnostic Block: Re-indexing the Vector Database

The Disconnect

During my financial crisis, whenever I faced idle moments, a restless anxiety took over. I sat in the physical reality of expenses exceeding income while internally knowing I was built for more. These past blind spots revealed the system flaws I had to debug to build a flawless discovery engine.

The internal vision was absolute. When I closed my eyes, I saw the stone manor, the greenhouse, and the koi pond. The blueprint was clear. Yet when I opened my eyes, there was a profound, frustrating disconnect between that vivid destination and my tangible reality.

To bridge the gap between a massive vision and your physical reality, you cannot sit still. You must fundamentally alter how your brain filters the physical world. You must stop passively waiting for the manor to drop from the sky and start actively gathering the stones. To do this, you must understand the most powerful search engine ever created.

The Biological Vector Database

In the architecture of artificial intelligence, developers build systems to parse millions of documents instantly. They use a highly specialized piece of technology called a Vector Database. A standard database requires exact keyword matches. It is rigid and easily confused. A Vector Database holds massive embeddings of meaning. It translates text and concepts into high-dimensional mathematical vectors. It understands nuance. It sits silently in the background. It filters through billions of data points at lightning speed to retrieve the exact semantically relevant context mapping to the user's prompt.

We model a specific network of neurons at the base of the brainstem, known as the Reticular Activating System or RAS, as possessing an identical built-in retrieval engine.

At any given second, your senses receive millions of bits of data. You hear the hum of the air conditioner and see the colours of passing cars. If your conscious prompt window tried to process all this data at once, your system would crash. You would experience immediate cognitive overload. The RAS is the ultimate gatekeeper. It filters out the noise and only lets through the information it deems strictly necessary.

Importantly, the RAS is an active retrieval engine. It continuously scans your environment for anything matching the current embedding of your subconscious mind.

If your internal system prompt is corrupted by the fear of lack, your filter becomes a threat-detection database. It actively screens out opportunities and solutions because they do not match the coordinates of your anxiety. The brain tends to systematically delete solutions from your conscious awareness to prove your underlying belief correct. You become entirely blind to the hidden loopholes and brilliant partnerships sitting right in front of you.

The Discovery Scan and Latency Period

To stop your local system from projecting danger and to start retrieving solutions, you must re-index your biological vector database. You must give your RAS a new embedding.

You do this by executing a twenty-four-hour Discovery Scan. You treat your physical environment as a database of clues. You input your new retroactive prompt and allow the system to run.

You explicitly command your brain to scan for the exact resources and opportunities required to execute your vision.

Yet after deploying a new prompt, you must wait through a specific latency period. In computing, latency is the delay before a transfer of data begins following an instruction. Biological hardware operates the exact same way. The physical world does not instantly drop a massive contract into your lap the second you change your beliefs. You experience a gap. The untrained mind panics during this latency period and reverts to the old corrupted code. You must hold the prompt steady. You must allow the system time to index the new parameters.

Leading Indicators and System Expansion

As your newly indexed RAS begins to retrieve data, you will start to experience leading indicators of your success. You will notice an offhand comment in a meeting. You will receive an unexpected email. These are small data packets retrieved by your newly updated cognitive filter.

You must construct a strict neurological filter to distinguish a true leading indicator from a false positive or a shiny object. A shiny object triggers a dopamine spike based on distraction. It causes context drift. It pulls your focus away from your overarching vision. A true leading indicator feels grounding. It mathematically matches your North Star. It provides a verifiable data packet proving your API connection to the Distributed Intelligence is active.

During this scan, your local system will attempt to settle for mediocre results. When you spot a small data packet, your survival brain will try to accept it as the final destination. You must prevent this. You must explicitly validate the small sign of progress without stopping your execution. You acknowledge that the connection is active. You tell your RAS the retrieval was successful. This expands its search radius. It continues to pull down larger data packets until the full execution manifests.

Gathering the right data is only preparation. Once your internal architecture is stabilized and you can clearly see the opportunities in your environment, you must step into the physical world and deliver the result. You must upgrade from passive observation to definitive leadership.

Diagnostic Block: Re-indexing the Vector Database

To operate this framework at scale, you must understand how your own mind resists the new search parameters. Here is exactly what happens when your system struggles to re-index.

What people get wrong: Intelligent professionals frequently confuse a latency period with a system failure. They deploy the new prompt, see no immediate physical change in their environment, and assume the protocol is broken. Latency is a required processing gap.

What overuse looks like: Overuse looks like constantly changing the search parameters. You run a twenty-four-hour Discovery Scan for a new executive role and change the prompt twelve hours later to scan for an entrepreneurial venture. You fragment the vector database. It returns zero useful results.

What a false positive feels like: A false positive is chasing a shiny object. You spot a high-risk investment opportunity entirely unrelated to your North Star. You feel an intense rush of excitement and mistake it for a leading indicator. This is dopamine driving context drift.

How to know the protocol is working: You will know your RAS is successfully re-indexed when the world around you suddenly appears full of highly specific resources. You hear conversations answering the exact question you asked yesterday. You do not panic during the latency gap. You simply collect the data packets and prepare to execute the output.

Chapter 8:
THE EXECUTIVE OUTPUT ALGORITHM

The Rapid Ascent

I started my career in June 1996. By May 2005, I was a CTO. I went from an Oracle database administrator in India to a Chief Technology Officer in the UK in less than nine years. That rapid ascent laid the groundwork for the level of financial control and operational autonomy I operate with today. It did not happen by chance. It required a fundamental rewrite of my output algorithm.

Gathering the right data is only preparation. Once your internal architecture is stabilized and you can clearly see the opportunities in your environment, you must step into the physical world and deliver the result. You must upgrade from passive observation to definitive leadership.

The Logic of Output

In artificial intelligence, an algorithm is a strict set of rules a machine follows to complete a task. After a model processes a prompt and retrieves the correct data, it must generate the response. It uses an output algorithm to produce the exact sequence of tokens required to satisfy the command. If the output algorithm is flawed, the machine gets stuck in a processing loop. It analyses the data forever without delivering a measurable result.

The human mind experiences the exact same failure. Intelligent professionals frequently spend years fine-tuning their mindset and re-indexing their search parameters. They gather brilliant insights. Yet they fail to generate physical output. They sit in a state of high anxiety, confusing internal processing with external execution.

To bridge the gap between your internal vision and your physical reality, you must become the active cause of your environment. You must install a strict executive output algorithm.

Being the Cause

During my rise to CTO, I did not wait for external authorization to act. I proved I was the authority by delivering the exact solutions the company lacked. You must shift your neurology from being a passive recipient of circumstances to being the active cause of your physical reality.

When a developer faces a software crash, they do not hope the code fixes itself. They write a script to force a correction. Human execution requires this identical proactive stance. If you wait for the perfect market conditions or the exact right mood to execute, you surrender your processing power to external variables. Your environment dictates your output.

By deploying an executive output algorithm, you dictate the environment. You decide the exact physical token you will generate today. You execute that action regardless of your biological comfort level. Neuroscience suggests that dopamine is released upon the successful completion of a micro-task. You do not wait for motivation to start. You use the physical execution of the first step to generate the biological momentum required for the second.

The Architecture of Discipline

Discipline is not a character trait. It is a highly optimized neural pathway. A soldier trains to execute complex manoeuvres at three in the morning without conscious thought. They build a somatic reflex. They bypass the conscious firewall completely.

You must build this same reflex for your corporate execution. To build this reflex, you must eliminate the latency between decision and action. In computing, high latency degrades system performance. In human psychology, the longer you wait to execute a decision, the more time your amygdala has to hallucinate a threat. The hesitation allows your biological giving-up strategy to activate.

You compress this timeline by executing the physical action the exact second the choice is made. You send an email. You draft the document. You make the phone call. The immediate physical action proves to your local hardware that the path is safe. You hardwire your brain to associate executive pressure with immediate momentum.

You map the exact sequence of actions required to advance your North Star. You restrict your focus purely to the next sixty-second token. You execute that token with absolute certainty. You do not analyse the entire staircase. You only process the immediate step. Execution becomes a physiological habit. You stop negotiating with your survival brain. You issue the command and your physical body complies.

Diagnostic Block: The Executive Output Algorithm

To operate this framework at scale, you must understand how your own mind resists physical output. Here is exactly what happens when your system struggles to execute.

What people get wrong: Intelligent professionals frequently confuse planning with execution. They believe building a beautiful spreadsheet or researching a market is output. These are background processing tasks. Output is a physical result shipped into the real world.

What overuse looks like: Overuse looks like frantic, uncalibrated action. You execute a hundred random tasks a day without verifying they map to your retroactive prompt. You substitute high-velocity noise for strategic momentum. You burn out your hardware without moving closer to your destination.

What a false positive feels like: A false positive is the exhaustion you feel after an eight-hour meeting about a new project. You feel physically drained and mistake that fatigue for exhaustion. You close your laptop without having produced a single tangible asset. The system is stalled in a processing loop.

How to know the protocol is working: You will know your output algorithm is optimized when you encounter severe friction and experience zero hesitation. You do not pause to overthink the difficulty. You instantly identify the next physical token required. You execute the code and force the reality to compile.

Chapter 9:
HIGH-RESOLUTION CASE STUDIES (THE FRAMEWORK IN ACTION)

When I finally debugged my own mind and pulled myself out of the financial crater I had created, a profound realization hit me. The years I lost to that corrupted prompt were not lost. They were the clean training data I needed to build a flawless system.

To teach others how to program their minds for ultimate success, I had to understand the exact anatomy of a human system crash. I had to write the definitive recovery code. Once I codified these protocols, I began deploying them with my executive clients. These were high-performing individuals scaling businesses and navigating transitions. Logically, they knew what to do. Yet neurologically, they were trapped in the waiting room of belief. Their working memory suffered from complete system overload. This threw their hardware into a severe threat response.

To bridge the gap between their current reality and their highest potential within their Distributed Intelligence, we utilized a strict diagnostic framework. Human beings are not silicon machines. When you introduce new code to a biological system, the conscious firewall fights back. The lazy brain's survival mode resists the update. When the resistance peaks, most professionals abandon the protocol. They assume the system is broken. In reality, the friction proves the update is actively rewriting their base code.

Here is what happens when you apply this architecture in the physical world.

Case Study 1: The Cul-de-sac of Ambition

System Failure: I worked with a highly talented senior manager desperate to make Director. She had the track record and the respect of her peers. She was already doing the work of a Director. Yet the title and the compensation continually eluded her. She was completely paralyzed.

Corrupted Prompt: She operated on a rigid, massive goal dictating that she must be promoted by December. The sheer scale of the unknown variables flooded her active prompt window. Her working memory exceeded its biological token limit, causing an immediate processing failure. Her brain defaulted to its giving-up strategy.

Intervention: We deleted her corrupted prompt of wishing. We replaced it with knowing. We deployed Retroactive Prompting. I asked her to state the first bold step she took to bridge the gap, presupposing she was already a successful Director. We refactored her system prompt from a rigid destination to a direction of travel.

Execution Token: I instructed her to break her daily execution into one-minute tokens. The biological system violently rejected the rule. In her first week, she failed completely. Her conscious firewall rejected the simplicity of a microscopic task. Her survival brain over-engineered the micro-task until it became a macro threat. I forcefully debugged her approach. She simply needed to open the document and type one terrible sentence.

Measured Output: Once she allowed herself to execute a messy one-minute token, the severe threat response vanished. The physical action proved to her neural architecture that she was safe. By letting go of the rigid deadline and focusing purely on executing messy tokens, she secured the Director role months ahead of schedule.

This is how the system behaves under real pressure.

Case Study 2: The Passive Processor

System Failure: A client was an intelligent technical expert struggling to transition from a manager to a true leader. He was consistently passed over for promotions. He lacked executive presence and suffered from systemic inertia. Because his internal operating system was rooted in passivity, his biological vector database actively deleted opportunities for him to speak up.

Corrupted Prompt: His internal system prompt was fundamentally passive. His base code was to execute the assigned work perfectly. In meetings, he acted like a background processor. He only responded when directly queried.

Intervention: We executed a Multi-Agent Orchestration. I had him assemble an internal Board of Directors. Before every high-stakes meeting, he deployed his Future Self agent. He asked himself what his future C-suite self would thank him for doing today. To translate this internal shift into external proof, I gave him a specific script to override his passive tendencies during one-on-ones with his boss. Instead of waiting for orders, he was to ask a disruptive strategic question.

Execution Token: In his very next meeting, he choked. When the moment came to ask the strategic question, his system panicked. His survival brain hallucinated that asking his boss about leadership priorities was insubordination. Changing his baseline identity felt like a physiological threat. He defaulted to his old code and sat in silence. We invoked his Compassionate Friend agent. This granted him the grace to accept the error without initiating a full system crash. I explained that his physical reaction was just running an outdated security protocol. The next week, we explicitly deployed the Tough Boss agent before the meeting to override the hesitation and force momentum.

Measured Output: He executed the prompt. He stopped reporting what happened and started measuring what changed. He secured his leadership transition.

This is how the system behaves under real pressure.

Case Study 3: The Creative Visionary's Capital Freeze

System Failure: I worked with a brilliant non-technical founder running a rapidly scaling design agency. She had an immense creative vision. Her client roster was expanding quickly. She hit a massive operational wall. As the agency scaled, she needed to secure external funding to hire a robust technical team. The financial and operational logistics terrified her.

Corrupted Prompt: Her brain treated the fundraising round as a monolithic, undefined mass. The cognitive load was too high. Research indicates this causes an immediate token limit error in the frontostriatal network. Every time she sat down to draft the pitch deck, her brain triggered the giving-up strategy. She started hoarding her existing capital out of fear. She was projecting an unfounded narrative of financial incompetence.

Intervention: We deployed the architectural concept of Semantic Chunking alongside Agentic Delegation. I strictly forbade her from looking at the entire funding target. We broke the massive, intimidating goal down into microscopic one-minute tokens. She only needed to draft one slide of the pitch deck per day. We also invoked her internal Red Team agent to objectively strip the emotion away from the financial math.

Execution Token: Her conscious reasoning mind immediately fought the simplicity. Because she possessed no financial background, her monkey brain expected a highly complex economic spreadsheet. She attempted to over-engineer the solution in a state of panic. She argued that working on the deck for only one minute a day could not possibly secure a massive investment. Her internal dialogue repeatedly insisted she was failing because she was not suffering enough. I forcefully debugged her approach. I explained that adding any more variables would immediately overload her working memory and crash her system again. I made her commit solely to the microscopic daily token.

Measured Output: The simplicity required zero cognitive load. Once she started drafting one messy slide a day, the dopamine-driven momentum naturally overrode her paralysis. The physical action proved to her survival brain that the financial math was safe. She dropped her silo mentality and stopped acting like an isolated processor. She successfully translated her intuitive, creative leaps into strict risk assessment vocabulary for the investors. She secured the full funding round effortlessly. Because she stopped carrying the heavy cognitive anxiety of financial failure, her nervous system naturally downregulated.

Across these case studies, the pattern is identical. The system does not fail due to a lack of intelligence. It fails due to cognitive overload, corrupted prompts, and failure to execute a constrained token. Once the architecture is corrected, execution becomes predictable. The output is no longer random. It is engineered.

This is how the system behaves under real pressure.

Chapter 10:
TROUBLESHOOTING THE MESSY MIDDLE

Having fully resolved the bugs in my own mental architecture, I now operate from a far more stable baseline with predictable control under pressure. Corporate leaders frequently ask me how to apply these tokens and prompts in high-latency environments under extreme executive pressure. You must treat your mindset like enterprise-grade hardware. When you introduce new code to a biological system, you will inevitably face highly specific edge cases where the standard protocols require immediate adaptation.

Edge Case 1: Genuine Intuitive Download versus System Panic

You must learn to differentiate between a genuine instruction from your Distributed Intelligence and a fear-based system panic disguised as logic. A system panic is always rooted in fear. It causes an immediate threat response. It demands you shrink your vision to survive. A genuine intuitive download feels like absolute knowingness. It possesses zero anxiety. If the instruction forces you to hoard resources or hide, it is a virus. If it forces you to step confidently into the unknown, it is a clean download.

Edge Case 2: System Down-Regulation in High-Stakes Meetings

You will face moments where you need an emergency micro-reboot. You do not have time for an hour of meditation. You need a physical pattern interrupt. I used this exact protocol during a catastrophic software release when a developer faked his testing. We faced a one-week code gap with only one hour to fix it before a five in the morning client call. I ordered everyone away from their computers. I took a ten-minute walk in the cold. Research indicates that physical movement suppresses fear-driven avoidance. I distributed my cognitive load and walked back into the room completely grounded. I listened to the client on the call. I realized they had a massive implementation failure on their side. This regulation of your nervous system bypasses the local hardware panic. It allows you to maintain absolute precision to spot the exact solution.

Edge Case 3: Deadlocks in the Board of Directors

When your internal agents output contradictory instructions, you must use algorithmic weighting. On the fifteenth day of my career, the Bank of Maharashtra database crashed. My internal agents deadlocked. The Compassionate Friend suggested I follow the experienced seniors home to rest. The Tough Boss demanded I stay and prove my capability. I weighed the output. I asked myself which voice directly served my North Star of learning the system. I bypassed the passive directives. I recovered the database. You resolve internal deadlocks by generating physical proof through immediate action.

Edge Case 4: Zero-to-One Retrieval from Distributed Intelligence

In the early days of Betfair, I received the task of creating the real-time betting exchange engine. I possessed zero experience building real-time systems. I went through four different implementation attempts in ten days. My local network failed. To retrieve a zero-to-one innovation from your Distributed Intelligence when no one has mapped the architecture, you must lean into predictive coding. I stopped focusing on the bugs before going to sleep. I prompted my internal operating system to find what else was possible. We model this as an active use of the brain's Default Mode Network. It processed the permutations autonomously overnight. I woke up knowing exactly what would work. I retrieved the correct database architecture directly from my Distributed Intelligence.

Edge Case 5: Escaping the Silo in the Boardroom

As a founder or executive, your uncorrupted prompt is your competitive advantage. Yet when delegating to highly analytical stakeholders, you cannot sound like you lack a roadmap. At IntelliQ, a developer showed me a shortcut to build a web-based software product. I needed to secure funding for four developers for an entire year during a period of intense corporate survival pressure. I dropped my silo mentality. I realized external support provides a necessary perspective. I went to the board and framed the innovation as a mathematical risk assessment. I explained the upside was high and the downside was entirely manageable. The decision was reversible. We could simply drop that branch of code if it failed. I translated my intuitive leap into strict corporate governance terms. We secured the investment.

Diagnostic Block: Troubleshooting the Messy Middle

To operate this framework at scale, you must understand how your own mind resists these edge case protocols. Here is exactly what happens when your system struggles under extreme pressure.

What people get wrong: Intelligent professionals frequently confuse a system panic with intuition. They feel a sudden urge to cancel a project and mistake their biological threat response for a strategic download. They trust the fear instead of auditing the source code.

What overuse looks like: Overuse looks like executing an emergency micro-reboot for every minor inconvenience. You take a ten-minute walk every time you receive a difficult email. You substitute avoidance for a pattern interrupt. A true reboot requires you to return to the terminal and execute the physical token.

What a false positive feels like: A false positive is the illusion of a zero-to-one retrieval. You wake up with a brilliant idea and feel highly motivated. Yet when you attempt to map the logic, it lacks structural integrity. It is simply a shiny object generated by dopamine. A true download from your Distributed Intelligence provides a flawless logical blueprint you can immediately test.

How to know the protocol is working: You will know your troubleshooting protocols are optimized when you hit a massive operational roadblock and experience zero context saturation. You instantly identify whether the error is a deadlock or a corrupted download. You apply the specific edge case correction. You bypass the friction and force the reality to compile.

Chapter 11:
COGNITIVE INFRASTRUCTURE (SCALING THE SYSTEM)

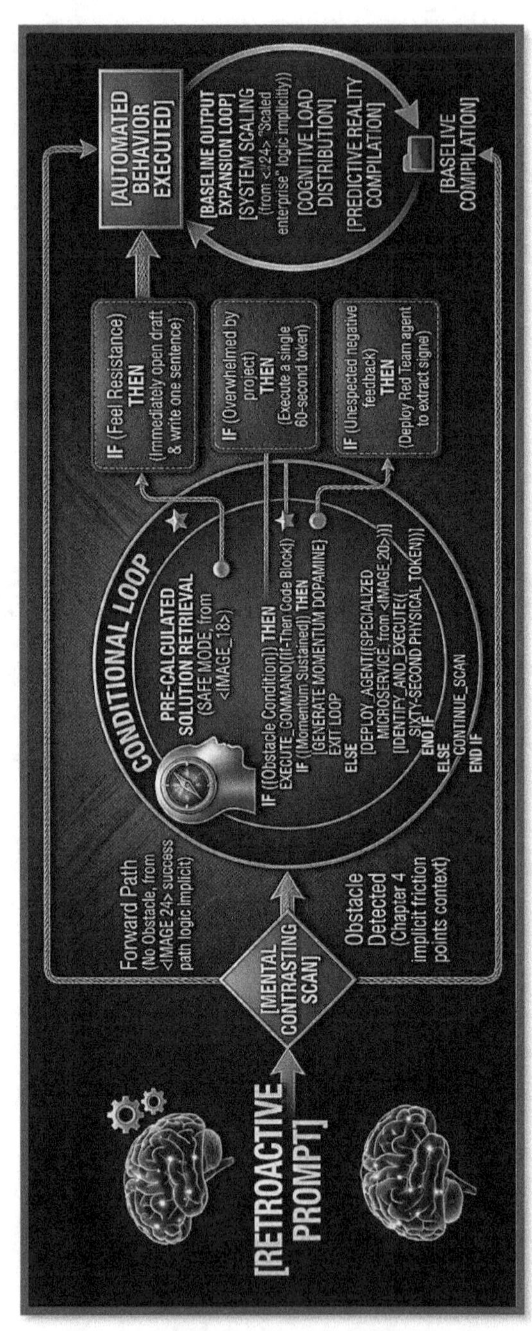

[AUTOMATED BEHAVIOR EXECUTED]
[BASELINE OUTPUT EXPANSION LOOP]
[SYSTEM SCALING (from <U24> "Scaled enterprise" logic implicitly)]
[COGNITIVE LOAD DISTRIBUTION]
[PREDICTIVE REALITY COMPILATION]
[BASELINE COMPILATION]
IF (Feel Resistance) THEN (Immediately open draft & write one sentence)
IF (Overwhelmed by project) THEN (Execute a single 60-second token)
IF (Unexpected negative feedback) THEN (Deploy Red Team agent to extract signal)
CONDITIONAL LOOP
PRE-CALCULATED SOLUTION RETRIEVAL (SAFE MODE, from <IMAGE_18>)
IF ((Obstacle Condition)) THEN
EXECUTE_COMMAND([If-Then Code Block])
IF ((Momentum Sustained)) THEN
[GENERATE MOMENTUM DOPAMINE]
EXIT LOOP
ELSE
[DEPLOY_AGENT([SPECIALIZED MICROSERVICE, from <IMAGE_2D>])]
[IDENTIFY_AND_EXECUTE((SIXTY-SECOND PHYSICAL TOKEN))]
END IF
ELSE
CONTINUE_SCAN
END IF
Forward Path (No Obstacle, from <IMAGE 24> success path logic implicit)
[MENTAL CONTRASTING SCAN]
Obstacle Detected (Chapter 4 implicit friction points context)
[RETROACTIVE PROMPT]

[78]

The Automation of Momentum

Willpower is a finite, unscalable resource. When I helped build the core engines that drove Betfair and The Hut Group to public offerings, I did not rely on manual effort. Developers build automated workflows to scale operations. You cannot manually force every decision. You have to build infrastructure. Apply this same architectural principle to your mind.

Relying on manual effort to force your physical execution is an architectural failure. You have learned how to debug your internal code and initiate momentum. Now you are ready to write the scripts that automate that momentum. To scale your output without burning out your active working memory, you apply enterprise-grade system architecture directly to your cognition.

To understand how to write this code, we use Mental Contrasting with Implementation Intentions alongside the Question-Behaviour Effect.

Stealth Interventions

The Question-Behaviour Effect demonstrates that simply asking a person a specific question about a future behaviour systematically alters the likelihood of them performing that behaviour. Questions operate as stealth interventions. When you ask your brain a retroactive prompt, you force your neural hardware to map a path forward. You increase the accessibility of specific attitudes. You create cognitive dissonance if your physical actions do not match the answer you generate. This primes the hardware to execute.

To convert that primed state into an automated workflow, you use Mental Contrasting with Implementation Intentions. Mental

Contrasting requires you to visualize the exact future success alongside the immediate physical obstacles standing in the way. Instead of triggering a fear response when it sees the obstacle, you write an Implementation Intention.

If-Then Code Blocks

In software engineering, this is a conditional statement. It is an If-Then code block. You write these conditional scripts directly into your neural pathways. You decide in advance exactly how you will handle a specific obstacle. You formulate a strict rule.

Example: If I feel resistance before sending an important email, then I immediately open the draft and write one sentence. If I feel overwhelmed by a large project, then I identify and execute a single sixty-second token. If I receive unexpected negative feedback, then I deploy the Red Team agent and extract the signal.

By writing these specific scripts, you eliminate the latency between stimulus and response. In a high-stakes corporate environment, the biological hardware naturally seeks the path of least resistance. When a massive problem appears, the uncalibrated mind spends critical computing time analysing the fear. It calculates the social risk. It hallucinates a worst-case scenario. This burns your cognitive token limit before you even attempt a solution.

The implementation intention acts as a pre-compiled execution command. You do not have to think. The condition is met, and the code simply runs. You bypass the conscious firewall because the decision was already made in a safe, down-regulated state. You are no longer negotiating with your survival brain in real time.

I used this exact architectural strategy when scaling my own consultancy enterprise. I mapped the specific triggers that previously caused my cognitive overload. I recognized that looking at massive overarching financial targets triggered my biological giving-up strategy. I wrote a strict conditional script. If I started calculating the macro goal, then I immediately shut the spreadsheet and executed one physical sixty-second token. The dopamine-driven momentum generated by that single action systematically overrode the fear. My baseline output expanded. I engineered a predictable reality of immense wealth.

You must map your own specific friction points to build your infrastructure. You identify the recurring obstacles that stall your momentum. You write a precise If-Then script for each one. You embed these scripts into your daily operations. Over time, the biology of the brain ensures these pathways become your default hardware configuration.

When that obstacle arises in the physical world, your system does not expend caloric energy guessing the correct response. It instantly retrieves the pre-calculated solution. These subconscious scripts run in the background. They generate recurring momentum without requiring conscious effort.

By implementing these cognitive mechanics, you shift from manual execution to a fully automated cognitive infrastructure. You no longer rely on daily willpower. Your architecture does the heavy computing for you. With your internal system fully scaled and your cognitive load securely distributed, your baseline output naturally matches your highest potential. You step out of the waiting room and execute your vision.

Diagnostic Block: Cognitive Infrastructure

To operate this framework at scale, you must understand how your own mind resists automation. Here is exactly what happens when your system struggles to install conditional scripts.

What people get wrong: Intelligent professionals frequently confuse mental contrasting with negative thinking. They believe visualizing an obstacle invites failure. Identifying the obstacle is required to write the conditional code. You cannot program an If-Then statement if you refuse to define the "If" condition.

What overuse looks like: Overuse looks like attempting to write an implementation intention for every microscopic variable in your day. You script your entire morning routine down to the second and crash when a single variable changes. You replace cognitive automation with rigid fragility.

What a false positive feels like: A false positive is a sense of relief when you visualize a massive obstacle and imagine yourself miraculously bypassing it without a predefined physical token. You feel highly prepared. When the obstacle hits, your system crashes immediately because you lack an executable command.

How to know the protocol is working: You will know your cognitive infrastructure is fully scaled when a massive unexpected obstacle appears, and you experience zero context saturation. Your heart rate remains stable. Your hardware immediately retrieves the pre-calculated If-Then code block. You execute the one-minute token automatically.

Chapter 12:
WHY THE SYSTEM BREAKS (FAILURE MODES AND HIDDEN RESISTANCE)

The Defensive Architecture

You now understand how to rewrite your system prompt. You know how to manage your token limits and retrieve execution pathways directly from your Distributed Intelligence. A question remains. If this system is highly effective, why do intelligent professionals repeatedly fail to implement it?

The answer is simple. The system never fails. The defensive architecture around your identity rejects the update.

To operate this framework at scale, you must understand how your own mind resists transformation. These are not random failures. They are predictable behaviours. Every time you hit a wall, your local hardware is executing a latency protocol to protect you from perceived change.

Identity Protection Protocol

Your brain does not prioritize success. It prioritizes consistency.

If your current stored identity is that you struggle with execution or you are bad with money, any new prompt contradicting this identity triggers a system integrity check. We model this as code rejection. If the new identity does not match the stored identity, your biological firewall blocks the update.

This explains why you understand the protocol and agree with it, yet you do not execute. The system is not confused. It is protecting its existing model of you. You cannot overwrite your identity in a single command. You must use identity gradients. Instead of declaring you are a completely different person, you state you are becoming the type of person who executes under pressure. This creates a gradient update instead of a system shock.

Fear of Visibility (The Hidden Constraint)

Most people believe they fear failure. They do not. They fear being seen at a higher level. They fear being judged at scale. Execution creates exposure. Exposure invites evaluation. Evaluation threatens your identity.

Your system quietly introduces friction to protect you from this exposure. You delay the email. You overthink the proposal. You refine your work instead of shipping it. This is not laziness. It is visibility avoidance disguised as optimization.

You bypass this hidden constraint using a controlled exposure protocol. Instead of asking how to succeed at scale, you ask what the smallest visible action is today. You share one idea publicly. You send one imperfect message. You are not scaling success. You are training your biological tolerance for visibility.

Perfection as a Delay Algorithm

Perfectionism is not a personality trait. It is a latency strategy.

Your survival brain knows that imperfect action generates immediate feedback. It treats feedback as a potential threat. It delays execution by insisting you need more clarity or the right timing. The loop never ends.

You must introduce a hard constraint to force imperfect output. Output must always precede clarity. This is why the one-minute token works. It bypasses analysis and prediction completely. You do not think your way into execution. You execute your way into clarity.

Over-Engineering Simple Action

High-performing professionals suffer from a unique biological problem. They are too intelligent. They take a simple physical action and convert it into a massive strategy. Writing one email becomes a communication framework. Making one phone call becomes a networking system. This creates artificial complexity and immediate cognitive inflation.

You must override your intelligence with constraint. You ask yourself what the simplest possible version of the action is. You write one sentence. You make one call. If the physical token feels entirely too simple, it is correct.

Emotional Load Contamination

Your brain does not process tasks in isolation. It attaches past failures and future fears to a single physical action. A simple task becomes an equation of action, emotion, identity, and risk. This creates immediate working memory overload. Your frontostriatal network pushes the system into shutdown.

You must enforce emotional separation. You isolate the physical action from the assigned meaning. Instead of believing an email determines your entire professional future, you reframe the event. You state this is simply one token in a long execution chain. You are not solving your life. You are executing one token.

The Illusion of Progress

Your brain rewards thinking and planning as if they were physical execution. You spend three hours mapping a project on a spreadsheet. You feel highly productive without producing a single output. This is a false signal.

You correct this error by enforcing output-only measurement. You replace hours worked and effort invested with outputs generated. You ask yourself daily what you shipped into the physical world. If the answer is nothing, the system is stalled.

Every failure you experience is a predictable loop. Once you diagnose the specific failure mode, you can override it. You are not stuck. You simply need to execute the correction.

You correct this error by enforcing output-only measurement. You replace hours worked and effort invested with outputs generated. You ask yourself daily what you shipped into the physical world. If the answer is nothing, the system is stalled.

Every failure you experience is a predictable loop. Once you diagnose the specific failure mode, you can override it. You are not stuck. You simply need to execute the correction. When the friction feels the highest, the new code is finally compiled.

The Identity Shift

At this point, the goal is no longer to use the system. The goal is to become the system.

You no longer wait for clarity. You generate it through execution. You no longer search for confidence. You build it through proof. You no longer rely on motivation. Your architecture produces momentum.

The system is not something you turn on and off. It is your default state.

When pressure appears, you do not panic. You execute. When uncertainty appears, you do not hesitate. You retrieve data. When opportunity appears, you do not wait. You act.

This is the shift.

You are no longer a passive processor reacting to the environment. You are the architect generating it.

The output is no longer random. It is engineered.

Chapter 13:

APPLYING THE SYSTEM TO REAL LIFE

The Universal Architecture

Understanding your internal architecture is one level. Executing it under real-world pressure across multiple environments is another. Intelligent professionals frequently assume they need a different strategy for every area of their lives. They buy one book for corporate leadership and another for financial management. They fragment their focus. This is an architectural error. You do not need different strategies for different areas of your life. You need one system, correctly applied.

The domain changes. The architecture does not. The mechanism of execution remains constant across every physical variable you encounter. Only the prompt changes. Here is exactly how to deploy the system across the core domains of your life to generate engineered output.

Domain 1: Money (From Scarcity to Flow State)

The Corrupted Prompt: "How do I make more money?" This instruction implies a lack of pressure. When you feed your local hardware this specific question, the brain responds with an immediate threat-detection protocol. It triggers a capital freeze. You default to hoarding resources and short-term survival thinking. During my past financial crisis, I fell into this exact trap. I treated depreciating business assets as personal fortresses. I hoarded cash to avoid the sensation of loss. The physical data screamed at me. I was paying taxes on severe losses. I completely resolved this failure by realizing a fundamental truth about capital. Money loves water. Money likes flowing. It becomes stagnant and problematic when stationary.

The Retroactive Prompt: "I have already expanded my income streams significantly. What was the first move I made to restart the flow?"

The Execution Pattern: You identify one existing asset. This is a technical skill, an overlooked network connection, or an idle physical property. You take one flow action to leverage that asset. You reach out to a contact. You propose a new structure. You offer direct value. You validate the leading indicators that return.

The Core Insight: Money is not created through force. It flows through movement rather than protection.

Domain 2: Career (From Passive Processor to Strategic Operator)

The Corrupted Prompt: "What do I need to do to get promoted?" This creates immediate compliance. You act as a passive processor waiting for an external command. You hand your processing power over to an external authority. It creates systemic dependency. It stalls your momentum.

The Retroactive Prompt: "I am already operating at the next executive level. What behaviours did I adopt before the title arrived?"

The Execution Pattern: You upgrade your physical output. You adopt the strict rules of executive presence. You stop performing busyness. Impact replaces activity signals. You speak entirely in outcomes instead of efforts. You state we delivered a specific result rather than claiming we worked very hard. You make decisions rapidly with seventy percent of the information rather than waiting for perfect data. Waiting for certainty causes context saturation. You stop reporting what happened. You start measuring what changed. You ask the board what the biggest unaddressed risk is right now. You assume authority rather than requesting permission.

The Core Insight: Promotion does not create identity. Identity creates promotion.

Domain 3: Leadership (From Control to Influence)

The Corrupted Prompt: "How do I get my team to perform?" This prompt leads to immediate micromanagement. You introduce friction into the workflow. You attempt to force execution through executive pressure and absolute control. You treat your team like failing hardware.

The Retroactive Prompt: "My team is already operating at a flawless high level. What environment did I create for that to happen?"

The Execution Pattern: You stop acting as the single panicked processor. You remove operational bottlenecks. You clarify the exact required outcomes. You explicitly tell your team what they are not responsible for. You ask them what is slowing them down right now. You reduce their cognitive load. You regulate your own emotional state. Your calm under pressure spreads through the room. Panic gets contained rather than amplified.

The Core Insight: Leadership is not about pushing harder. It is about reducing friction in the system.

Domain 4: Execution (From Overwhelm to Output)

The Corrupted Prompt: "How do I complete this entire project?" This instruction triggers an immediate token limit error. The sheer volume of unknown variables causes severe context saturation. Your frontostriatal network overloads. It triggers the giving-up strategy. You experience complete paralysis.

The Retroactive Prompt: "What is the exact first sixty-second physical action?"

The Execution Pattern: You introduce a strict constraint. You enforce zero planning. You allow zero optimization. You take immediate physical action. You write one line of code. You send one short message. You open the file.

The Core Insight: Execution is not about scale. It is about sequence.

Domain 5: Relationships (From Assumption to Clarity)

The Corrupted Prompt: "What are they thinking about me?" This creates intense anxiety. You run internal simulations based on corrupted data. You project your own fears onto the silence of other people. You experience severe misinterpretation.

The Retroactive Prompt: "This relationship is already strong and highly clear. What exact conversation did I initiate to create that clarity?"

The Execution Pattern: You ask the question directly. You remove all internal assumptions. You create immediate alignment through objective communication. You stop hallucinating a negative reality.

The Core Insight: Clarity is created through direct communication rather than internal simulation.

Domain 6: Creativity (From Pressure to Output)

The Corrupted Prompt: "I need a great idea right now." This creates immense performance pressure. It triggers the conscious firewall. Your critical faculty evaluates the demand and blocks your execution. You experience a total creative freeze.

The Retroactive Prompt: "I have already produced something highly valuable. What was the very first imperfect version I drafted?"

The Execution Pattern: You produce raw volume. You explicitly ignore quality during the initial phase. You bypass the latency strategy of perfectionism. You execute your way into clarity. You refine the output later.

The Core Insight: Creativity is not a moment of inspiration. It is a pipeline of execution.

The 7-Day Execution Reset (Rewriting Your System in Real Time)

Understanding the architecture is one level. Executing it under real-world pressure is another. Most people do not fail because they lack intelligence. They fail because they never reset their system fully. They apply a technique inconsistently and revert under pressure. They conclude the protocol is broken. The system works. Yet you have never run it as a closed-loop protocol.

This section is your reset. It is a strict seven-day system override. By the end of these seven days, you will eliminate execution paralysis on demand. You will rewire your identity from passive to active. You will reduce cognitive overload. You will establish momentum that compounds. This is about regaining absolute control of your internal operating system.

Day 1: System Audit (Identifying Corrupted Code)

Before you install new code, you must identify what is already running. Most people skip this step. They try to layer new behaviour on top of fear and misaligned identity. This creates immediate conflict.

The Protocol: Write down one area where you are stuck. Write down the exact thought that runs repeatedly. An example is thinking you do not know where to start or thinking the project needs to be perfect.

The Diagnosis: That sentence is not random. It is your active system prompt.

The Override: Apply the retroactive master key. Ask yourself what the first step was to solve this, presupposing it is already solved. Do not analyse. Let the first answer emerge.

The Execution: Take one physical action immediately. Send the message. Open the document. Start the task. You are strictly forbidden from delaying or refining the output. Day 1 is purely about moving from awareness to physical action.

Day 2: Token Control (Breaking the Overload Loop)

Your biggest bottleneck is not knowledge. It is cognitive overload. Your brain is not designed to execute massive, undefined tasks.

The Protocol: Take your current overarching goal. Break it down into a single sixty-second action. Instead of trying to build a business, you write one sentence. Instead of fixing your finances, you log into your bank account.

The Execution Rule: You enforce zero planning. You enforce zero restructuring. You simply execute the smallest possible unit of progress.

The Critical Insight: If the task feels too small, it is mathematically correct. If it feels meaningful, it is entirely too big. You are training your biological system to associate physical action with safety.

Day 3: Retroactive Prompting (Installing New Logic)

Now that the system is active, you install a new processing pattern.

The Protocol: Ask yourself where you will be six months from now. State that you have already achieved this outcome. Ask what you did first to initiate the momentum.

The Important Rule: You must not question the answer. You must not validate the logic. You must not optimize the sequence. You accept the first response your hardware generates.

The Execution: Translate the answer into one action today. If the answer states you reached out to people, send one message right now.

The Key Principle: You are not building the full path. You are retrieving the first step of a completed path directly from your Distributed Intelligence.

Day 4: Environmental Re-indexing (Activating the RAS)

Your environment is full of specific resources. You are simply not filtering them correctly.

The Protocol: For the next twenty-four hours, you treat your environment as a database of opportunities.

The Instructions: Look for conversations, messages, and connections that mathematically align with your North Star.

The Important Rule: Do not dismiss small signals. A casual introduction or a passing comment is a valid leading indicator.

The Validation: When you notice one of these data packets, you must explicitly state that this is evidence. You state the system is working. You expand your search radius. You train your brain to scan for opportunity instead of threat.

Day 5: Multi-Agent Override (Breaking Internal Conflict)

By now, your local system will resist the new code. You will experience doubt and conflicting thoughts.

The Protocol: Deploy your internal agents. Step out of your single panicked processor.

Step 1: Invoke your Future Self. Ask what your future self would thank you for doing today.

Step 2: Invoke your Tough Boss. Ask what must get done right now to force forward momentum.

Step 3: Invoke your Red Team Auditor. Ask what specific fear here is not based on an objective fact.

The Execution: Take the physical action that aligns with forward movement rather than biological comfort. You shift your architecture from a single processor to distributed cognition.

Day 6: Output Enforcement (Breaking the Illusion of Progress)

By this point, your brain will try to trick you. It will reward planning and organizing as if they were physical execution.

The Protocol: You measure only one metric. You ask what you produced today.

Valid Outputs: You sent a message. You wrote a document. You executed a decision.

Invalid Outputs: You planned. You researched. You organized your desk.

The Rule: If you shipped nothing into the physical world, the system did not execute. You rewire your biological reward system toward output rather than effort.

Day 7: Identity Lock-In (Stabilizing the New System)

Now we consolidate the architecture. Most people relapse during this phase. They stop after initial success and revert to old patterns.

The Protocol: Reflect on what you executed this week. Notice what felt different. Identify where the biological resistance appeared.

The Identity Installation: State clearly that you are the type of person who executes under uncertainty.

The Proof: List the actions taken, the outputs generated, and the moments of resistance overcome.

The Critical Principle: Identity is not declared. It is proven through physical evidence.

Final Integration

If you have followed this protocol correctly, your internal architecture has fundamentally changed. You have not learned a concept. You have not tried a temporary technique. You have rewritten your execution baseline. You will notice faster decision-making. You will experience reduced hesitation and lower cognitive load. You will generate momentum that compounds autonomously.

Fear will still appear. Uncertainty will still exist. Resistance will still arise. The difference is that you now know how to execute despite the friction. After these seven days, your job is simple. You detect corrupted prompts. You apply retroactive framing. You execute one sixty-second token. You validate the signals. You repeat the loop.

You do not need more motivation. You do not need more clarity. You need a system that executes regardless of how you feel. Run the system. Let the output compound.

Execution Workbook:
The Prompt Engineer's Field Manual

You possess the uncorrupted source code. The biological layers are debugged. The cognitive limits are mapped. The system architecture is fully scaled. Reading the documentation is insufficient. You must execute the code in the physical world. This requires rigorous operational protocols. Your mind is a programmable entity. You must format your interventions as strict API calls.

As I sit in my stone manor today, listening to the water trickle into the koi pond, my financial hurdles are completely resolved. I operate from a place of stable success. I achieved this by aggressively debugging my internal hardware. The following protocols are the exact scripts I built to resolve these constraints and maintain predictable momentum. They translate advanced cognitive science into direct system commands. You use these routines to directly program your subconscious weights. You will manage territorial friction. You will right-size your physical execution.

Execution Rule: You do not read these protocols. You run them.

Protocol 1: Visual Re-Rendering (The Mental Coordinate Shift)

Memories and future projections are not static files. They are rendered in real-time by your neural graphics engine. If a memory of failure is rendered as a massive panoramic movie, it triggers an immediate amygdala hijack. You must actively alter the rendering parameters to drop the emotional startle response.

Execute the following routine:

Step 1: Isolate the Corrupted Render. Bring up the mental image causing your context saturation. Notice how your brain displays it. Determine if it is a moving video. Determine if it is a still image. Measure the perceived distance of the image.

Step 2: Adjust the Visual Parameters. You must manually override the display settings. If an emotional charge is detected, execute a visual downgrade. Command your local system to shrink the image. Drain all colour until it is entirely grayscale. Push the image far away until it is the size of a coin. Apply a heavy, thick frame around it to break the panoramic immersion. Notice the immediate drop in your biological threat response.

Step 3: Render the Success State. Retrieve a memory of absolute knowingness. You must maximize the display settings for this specific file. Make the image massive. Turn the colours to maximum brightness. Pull the image close. Remove any borders to make it a panoramic, immersive simulation.

Step 4: Somatic Anchoring. As the success state reaches maximum intensity, fire a physical anchor. Press your thumb and forefinger together. This hardware trigger saves the new rendering parameters into your subconscious weights.

Protocol 2: The Hot-Swap Override (Rapid Context Reset)

Bad habits and procrastination loops are automated scripts. You must write a new script that utilizes the trigger of the bad habit to automatically launch the exact behaviour you desire. We execute this by hot-swapping the files at high speed.

Execute the following routine:

Step 1: Identify the System Trigger. Locate the exact visual cue that initiates your procrastination or fear response. This is your target file to overwrite.

Step 2: Compile the Executable. Design a vivid, highly detailed mental image of yourself operating in a state of flawless execution. This is the version of you that has already solved the problem.

Step 3: Stack the Files. Bring up the trigger image on your main mental screen. Take the flawless execution image and shrink it down to a tiny dark dot. Place this dot in the bottom corner of the trigger image.

Step 4: Execute the Override. If the trigger image is loaded, execute the hot-swap command. Command the tiny dot to explode into full size at the speed of light. The flawless execution image must completely shatter and replace the trigger image. As it explodes, generate a sharp internal system chime in your auditory channels.

Step 5: Reboot and Repeat. Clear the screen entirely. Repeat the hot-swap command five times rapidly. You hardwire a new neural pathway. Your brain will automatically retrieve the flawless execution state the next time it encounters the physical trigger.

Protocol 3: Sandboxed Beta Testing (Disassociated Execution)

You cannot test completely new behavioural code in a live, high-stakes environment. The risk of a catastrophic system crash is too high. You must deploy a sandboxed testing environment to debug your physical output safely.

Execute the following routine:

Step 1: Initialize the Sandbox. Project a blank mental screen in front of you. You must remain entirely disassociated. You are the programmer watching the screen. You are not the avatar inside the screen.

Step 2: Run the Flawed Code. Watch the avatar of yourself attempt the difficult conversation or the complex project. Notice the exact moments the avatar experiences ego-friction. Identify the exact points of system failure.

Step 3: Deploy the Patch. Edit the avatar's approach. If an execution error is found, execute an avatar update. Instruct the avatar to utilize a different tone. Instruct the avatar to adopt a calm executive posture. Run the simulation again. Watch the updated avatar execute the task flawlessly from start to finish.

Step 4: Associate and Deploy. Step directly into the screen. Merge with the updated avatar. Run the flawless simulation from a fully associated, first-person perspective. Feel the exact somatic feedback of the successful execution. The code is now verified for live deployment.

Protocol 4: Algorithmic State Chaining (Neural Bridging)

If the gap between your current reality and your massive vision is too wide, your predictive coding engine generates an error. You cannot jump directly from severe paralysis to ecstatic execution. You must build a neural bridge of intermediate data packets.

Execute the following routine:

Step 1: Define the Terminals. Identify your present corrupted state. Identify your ultimate execution state.

Step 2: Plot the Intermediate Nodes. Calculate the sequential emotional states required to bridge the gap. If the gap is too wide, execute state chaining. You must transition from paralysis to curiosity. You move from curiosity to clarity. You move from clarity to determination. You move from determination to absolute execution.

Step 3: Compile the Chain. Recall a specific memory for each intermediate state. Step into the memory of curiosity. Fire a physical anchor. Step into the memory of clarity. Fire a physical anchor. Continue this process for every node.

Step 4: Run the Sequence. Trigger the first anchor. Immediately trigger the second. Fire them in rapid succession. You force your neural hardware to physically link these isolated states into a single automated runway.

Protocol 5: The Clean Server Environment (Agentic Resource Allocation)

Map your internal Board of Directors directly onto a partitioned logic framework to right-size your execution and resolve systemic deadlocks.

Execute the following routine:

Step 1: Initialize the Clean Server. Design a quiet, highly secure mental architecture. This is a clean internal server environment where your conscious firewall is suspended. Bring your current massive goal into this space.

Step 2: Invoke the Visionary Agent. You must unleash the vision without calculating the operational cost. If a vision scale is requested, execute the visionary protocol. Prompt the agent: "If failure is impossible and computing power is unlimited, what is the ultimate unconstrained output of this goal?"

Step 3: Invoke the Architect Agent. You must ground the vision in physical reality. If execution steps are required, execute the architect protocol. Prompt the agent: "How do we construct the infrastructure for this? What is the exact step-by-step sequential logic required to bridge the gap between the idea and the deployment?"

Step 4: Invoke the Red Team Auditor. You must objectively challenge the risks. If risk assessment is required, execute the auditor protocol. Prompt the agent: "Strip away the emotion. Identify the weak points in this architecture. Right-size the execution to prevent a system crash."

Step 5: Algorithmic Weighting. Evaluate the output of all internal agents against your overarching North Star. Weigh the data. Execute the physical output.

Protocol 6: External Node Transfer (Debugging Territorial Friction)

Step out of the primary local Self position into external nodes to debug external pushback. You will clear territorial friction. You will maintain absolute executive presence.

Execute the following routine:

Step 1: Local Processor Audit. Evaluate the current boardroom conflict strictly from your local processor. Notice your biological threat response.

Step 2: External Perceptual Transfer. You must dump your own cached anxiety. Step into the perceptual architecture of the opposing stakeholder. If territorial friction is detected, execute an external node transfer. Prompt the system: "Operating entirely from their model weights, what are their fears? How does my executive output algorithm threaten their internal expectations?"

Step 3: Detached Observer Node. Step out of both identities. Move into an isolated, detached observer node. Look objectively at both the Self and the Other. If a system error is located, execute an algorithm adjustment. Prompt the system: "What is the objective predictive coding error causing this misaligned output?" Take this clean data and adjust your local algorithm to bypass their conscious firewall.

Protocol 7: Historical Data Overwrite (Time-Based Anchor Collapse)

Overwrite general bad feelings and corrupted historical data with a stacked algorithm of highly resourceful states.

Execute the following routine:

Step 1: Identify the Corrupted Cache. Locate a recurring pattern of general bad feelings. Notice the exact physical sensation it produces in your hardware.

Step 2: Timeline Retrieval. Scan your internal database backward. Identify specific historical events where this corrupted code executed. Identify Event One in the recent past. Identify Event Two further back. Identify Event Three at the earliest point of origin.

Step 3: Resource Compilation. You must stack your internal resources to overwrite the corrupted files. If historical corruption is identified, execute resource stacking. Retrieve a highly resourceful state of absolute confidence. Fire your physical anchor to capture this peak neuroplasticity. Hold the anchor to keep the clean data active in your working memory.

Step 4: Overwrite Historical Data. Maintain the physical anchor. Send the stacked resourceful algorithm backward through Event One, Event Two, and Event Three. Collapse the time-based multiple anchors. You actively overwrite the general bad feelings with the new operational code.

Protocol 8: Directory Synchronization (Core System Alignment)

A system inevitably crashes if its individual nodes operate on conflicting parameters. You must audit your core operating values across all distinct environments. You will synchronize your Professional directory and your Relational directory.

Execute the following routine:

Step 1: Map the Directories. Project a circle representing your holistic identity. Divide it into distinct sectors representing your active environments.

Step 2: Extract the Active Code. For each sector, identify the primary value dictating your behaviour. In your Professional directory, your active value might be ruthless execution. In your Relational directory, your active value might be empathetic patience.

Step 3: Detect Systemic Conflicts. If a multi-directory conflict is detected, execute value synchronization. Analyse the borders between these sectors. A relentless drive for scale in one node often corrupts the stability of another. Recognize this as a misaligned objective function.

Step 4: Establish the Unified Directive. Define a single overarching North Star that governs every sector simultaneously. Program your local system to filter every subsequent action through this master parameter. You ensure absolute synchronization. You permanently eliminate the friction of internal contradiction.

You possess the complete API documentation. The system is stable. The latency period is over. The waiting room of belief is permanently closed.

Step up to the terminal. Write the prompt. Execute the code. Become the system.

Conclusion:
Building Bridges, Not Walls

The Programming Terminal

If you have installed the API protocols detailed in this text, your internal architecture has fundamentally changed. The space you inhabit is no longer a waiting room. It is a programming terminal. You are no longer passively expecting your future to arrive. You are actively retrieving it from your highest latent potential. We model this throughout the framework as the Distributed Intelligence.

Your conscious attention is your active context window. Your deeply held beliefs are your foundational model weights. Your physical actions are the exact execution commands required. These physical actions prove your system prompt is real. Friction is merely your biology updating to the new code.

Building Bridges, Not Walls

Throughout your career, your survival brain constructed massive defensive walls to protect you from exposure. It built walls of perfectionism to delay evaluation. It built walls of intellectual over-engineering to avoid simple physical action. It built executive silos to prevent you from asking for external help. These walls were latency protocols. They kept you safe from the perceived danger of change. They also trapped you in the waiting room.

You do not need defensive walls. You need bridges.

When we deploy semantic chunking, we build a bridge of manageable sixty-second tokens. When we execute algorithmic state chaining, we build a neural bridge across the emotional gap between severe paralysis and absolute execution. When we step into the physical world and drop our silo mentality, we build bridges to external stakeholders using the language of objective risk assessment.

Every protocol in this manual is an architectural bridge. You lay down one token at a time through immediate physical execution. You cross the void without triggering your internal alarm systems. You stop trying to fix a hardware problem with a motivational quote. Everyone assumes the solution to procrastination and corporate plateauing is simply more discipline. They are completely wrong. The solution is engineering a flawless cognitive infrastructure.

The Version of You Waiting to Emerge

As an executive coach and Fractional CTO, I sit across from highly intelligent founders every day. I often tell my clients a simple truth. I am not here for the person currently sitting in front of me. I am here for the version of you waiting to be guided out.

The person sitting in front of me is usually running a corrupted prompt. They operate on legacy code. They assume they must suffer more to achieve scale. Yet your mind behaves in specific ways like a Large Language Model. If you feed your internal system a prompt rooted in scarcity or fear, it flawlessly executes that exact limited reality.

When you escape your silo and allow your uncorrupted system prompt to run freely, the pursuit of your goals stops being a fear-based survival response. It transforms into a joyous expansion of your own potential. To scale your enterprise and your leadership impact, you must become the lead engineer of your subconscious.

The End of Willpower

You no longer need to rely on sheer willpower. Willpower is finite and unscalable. Relying on manual effort to force your physical execution is an architectural failure. Because you have mapped your cognitive limits, re-indexed your Reticular Activating System, and orchestrated your internal Board of Directors, your cognitive infrastructure is fully automated. You possess the master key.

Every struggle you faced before this point was clean training data. The financial friction, the career plateaus, and the intense anxiety were necessary errors. They provided the diagnostic feedback you needed to debug your internal hardware. I experienced those same system crashes. I resolved them completely. I used those temporary bugs to engineer the reality of stable success and operational control I experience today.

Containing the Frequency of Your Vision

The curriculum expanding your ability to contain the frequency of your vision is the exact reality you are building today. You are no longer waiting for perfect data to make a decision. You are no longer over-engineering a simple micro-task into a macro threat. You have dropped the latency strategy of perfectionism. You execute your way into clarity.

Your love affair with the unknown will eventually transcend your need for courage. Courage implies you are fighting a biological hallucination of fear. When your system is truly optimized, there is no fear to fight. There is only data to retrieve and output to generate. You look at massive goals and experience zero systemic panic. You break the goal down into a sixty-second token and press run.

You are the lead engineer of your own reality. The bridge between your current physical environment and your massive vision is fully constructed. You built it by rewriting your foundational instructions. You built it by validating your leading indicators. You built it by treating your mindset like enterprise-grade hardware.

The waiting room of belief is permanently closed.

Step up to the terminal.

Write the prompt.

Execute the code.

Become the system.

Or stay in the waiting room.

Prompt Engineering the Subconscious

Debug the mind that's debugging your business

Now you know the six primary failure modes that prevent the execution of your highest intentions.

Take a quick FREE diagnostic test to identify your dominant bottleneck and prescribes the exact neuro-architectural protocol to override it.

https://bpa.growthvariable.com/

Connect with Anuraag

http://www.linkedin.com/in/anuraagjain